PANIC

*The Course of
a Psychoanalysis*

PANIC
The Course of
a Psychoanalysis

THORKIL VANGGAARD, M.D.

JENS VANGGAARD, PH.D.
Translator

W·W·Norton & Company · New York · London

The author and the translator express their gratitude to Mrs. Grace Goldin of Philadelphia for her generous help in revising the translation.

Copyright © 1987, 1989 by Thorkil Vanggaard

Published simultaneously in Canada by Penguin Books Canada Ltd., ⸳ 2801 John Street, Markham, Ontario L3R 1B4.

Printed in the United States of America.

First Edition

Library of Congress Cataloging-in-Publication Data

Vanggaard, Thorkil, 1910–
  [Angst. English]
  Panic : the course of a psychoanalysis / Thorkil Vanggaard ;
  translator, Jens Vanggaard. — 1st ed.
    p. cm.
  Translation of: Angst.
  "A Norton professional book."
  Includes index.
  1. Psychoanalysis—Case studies. 2. Panic attacks—Treatment—
  Case studies. I. Title.
  [DNLM: 1. Fear. 2. Panic. 3. Psychoanalytic Therapy. WM 178
  V253a]
  RC509.8.V3613   1989
  616.85′223—dc20
  DNLM/DLC   89-3324
  for Library of Congress   CIP

ISBN 0-393-70086-0

W. W. Norton & Company, Inc., 500 Fifth Avenue, New York, N.Y. 10110
W. W. Norton & Company Ltd., 37 Great Russell Street, London WC1B 3NU

1 2 3 4 5 6 7 8 9 0

Contents

ABOUT THIS BOOK

The following is the course of the psychoanalytical treatment of a man—*A*—who suffered from attacks of neurotic panic. It is now more than 17 years since treatment began, and more than 16 years since it ended with his cure. He has had no relapse. With minor exceptions, which are explained below, my account is identical with the case record which I kept, dictating it after the close of each session as soon as *A* had left.

I have had the case record in my keeping for all these years, unread by anyone but myself. It cannot be denied that time and again I have wished that it were possible to make it public. From a professional as well as a human point of view it must claim the interest of those who are alive to the workings of human nature behind mere outward behavior. Add to this that in the entire professional literature we have no day-to-day accounts, describing the course of a psychoanalysis, which make clear on what data the stated conclusions are based. This has also been stressed by other authors.* However, in this account every premise is stated ahead of the conclusions drawn from it; and, since this is a case record kept from session to session, no premise has been added in hindsight on the basis of the conclusions.

As time wore on and it gradually became clear how durable the result of the treatment was, this naturally contributed to my harboring the secret wish that publication might be possible at some point. Although faced with this temptation, throughout the years I stubbornly refused to yield to it. Obviously, reproduction of an analytical process would have to contain material so personal and private that, for reasons of discretion, it could not be laid open to the public.

I was thus steadfast in my resolve. But some months ago I again came across my case record, not having seen it for years. I reread it. Once more I was struck by the documentary value I could not help but feel it had. On the basis of this text, the nature of a psychoanalytical process could be described and demonstrated as it unfolds from session to session.

Furthermore, the account has been chosen neither because of the interest of the psychic material which emerged during the treatment nor because of the therapeutic results. Obviously both were unknown to me

*See, for instance R. J. Stoller, professor of psychiatry at the University of California, Los Angeles, and a psychoanalyst: "Despite the importance of discovering the psychodynamic sources of human behavior, and the extensiveness of the literature to date, there is not a single report in which the conclusions are preceded by the data that led to them." (*Splitting*, Introduction, p. XIII; New York: Dell, 1974).

when, after my first session with A, I decided to keep a detailed record on his case. Of course, a prerequisite for my decision was the feeling that this was a man with whom I could work. Such a feeling I have had with many patients, always without knowing whether or not I could rely on it. It is equally obvious that at the close of one session I could not know what the next would bring.

The analysis of A is the only one I have ever recorded in such systematic detail. Generally speaking this is too taxing. Over the years I could have done the same with quite a number of patients and could have given parallel accounts of their cases in regard to clarity of material, succinctness of the progress report, and quality of result. In this sense A is chosen at random.

Certain aspects of the current public debate might well call for renewed reflection on the desirability of publication. Nowadays, points of view are sharply divided as to the correct treatment of psychic illness, among the general public as well as teachers, psychologists, and doctors, psychiatrists included. Some are wholehearted partisans of psychotherapy as the only legitimate treatment, some of these, besides, advocating interference with the personal environment of the patients and reforms in society at large. They regard drugs as poison, serving only the convenience of doctors and the profit of the drug industry. Also, they regard it as unethical to treat people with pills instead of giving them a chance of improvement by working on themselves. In the other camp we find an equally firm conviction that the solution to the psychiatrist's therapeutic problems is to be found in the field of chemistry. Those so convinced base their conviction on experiences with the use of the latest psychopharmacological drugs, especially the excellent ones for (endogenous) depression, which are now available to us, thanks to the diligent and competent efforts of the drug industries. Among the partisans of the latter view may be found many influential psychiatrists all over the world who even deny the existence of the category of neurosis. The two schools are in a state of total and implacable disagreement.

But a third party does exist, one which prefers to walk the middle road. This is where I belong. We of this party not only believe but claim that we *know* that some psychiatric illnesses, among them depressions, *must* be treated with drugs, while other kinds *must* be treated with psychotherapy. In the latter group a person like *A* belongs; given some drugs he would not benefit but only experience intolerable side-effects; given others he would fall victim to addiction. We also believe it to be unethical not to give such persons the chance to liberate themselves from their misery by working on their internal conflicts themselves, as well as the chance to benefit from the development of their personalities, which they can thus achieve.

At the moment the "psychopharmacological," i.e., drug-oriented, fraction has the upper hand, and its therapeutic principles tend to spread from their natural domain into that native to psychotherapy. Fighting this tendency is just as important as resisting the superstitious and harmful fear of drugs which prevails in the opposing camp.

Weighing all these factors, I finally felt I had to reappraise the question and maybe revise my decision. Of course, whatever my reasons, publication was unthinkable without the willing consent of *A*. Consequently I ventured to write to him, asking if he would be willing to read the case record and, given that he would, whether he would consider the possibility of finding some form in which it could be published—under necessary

[10]

disguise, of course. The disguise would, however, have to leave the essential analytical material and process untouched.

A's answer was truly obliging. Not only was he willing to read the case record, but he would also take time off to go over it thoroughly and make the alterations necessary to mask his identity. These proved to be far less extensive than I had expected. Names have been replaced by meaningless initials, places and dates are not to be accepted at face value, and certain facts and circumstances have been twisted without, however, changing them in principle, especially not in a way which would distort the picture painted of the personality of A and the process of his analysis. Thus, credit for the alterations is due to A.

As to alterations on my part, I have only removed a few redundant expressions, where they had slipped into my dictation. Apart from this, the text remains as it was dictated originally to my secretary, with no attempt made at emendation.

With A's permission Joseph Welner, M.D., professor of psychiatry, University of Copenhagen, read the original report and says: "I can affirm that no other alterations have taken place than the slight "veiling" which A made himself and which are of no significance whatsoever for the description of the course of the analytical process."

Thus, I may state that the following account presents a truthful picture of the course of the analysis, of A, and of my own role: the whole truth, that is, as I saw it at the time and still see it retrospectively. It should be added that A does not find my account in any way distorted.

Moreover, in addition to the effort he put into working over my report, A wished to comment on it himself and to relate what has happened since.

I would here add a few words of orientation about analytical method as I have practiced it, in accordance with the teaching in the Freudian tradition I received at The New York Psychoanalytic Institute during four years of training, coupled with my own experience throughout many years of practice since then.

The analytical situation is a relationship between two persons only—and in dealing with neurotic personalities it must be maintained as such. Thus I did not include anyone close to *A* in the treatment, for instance by meeting or interviewing them. I also had to demand of the analysand that he refrain from speaking to his relatives about what went on during analytical sessions. (*In casu* this especially applied to *A*'s wife.) The reason for this is that, were he to do so, it would have a disturbing effect upon the analytical process—if in no other way, by setting limits to what he would tell me of his family, should he have to be called to account at home for what he had said.

The analysand lies on a couch, the analyst sits behind him. In this way the situation is divested of the face-to-face character of normal verbal intercourse. It also frees both parties involved from the feeling of being constantly observed. The analysand is thus able to let his thoughts flow more freely, and the analyst may in a more relaxed manner listen and respond to his own introspective reactions on what he hears.

I never take notes during an analytical session. It would be distracting to me, and also, I believe, to my analysands. When, as in this case, I dicate immediately after each session, I believe my memory to be satisfactory, often even verbatim.

A session lasts 45 minutes.

As to the rest, my account will demonstrate the procedure, and in some final annotations I shall briefly stress certain points and add some explanatory remarks.

The Course of
the Analysis

September 16, 1969

A—a 44-year-old doctor, employed at a hospital in a superior capacity—came to me referred by the psychiatric consultant who had examined him at the department of medicine where he had been admitted with complaints of heart trouble. *A* described his troubles as follows:

Two and a half months ago he woke up suddenly one night with a feeling of dread, connected with palpitations and shortness of breath. He felt so panic-stricken that he was taken to a hospital. Cardiac examination gave a negative result as far as organic disease was concerned. This comforted him.

Reports from the hospital, where *A* had been admitted twice, from July 3rd to 8th, 1969 and from September 6th to 10th, 1969 read as follows on his first discharge:

> 44-year-old male, admitted on account of an acute outbreak of palpitations, dyspnea, and feelings of panic; earlier in his life he had experienced light precordial pressure, not related to exertion. He is overworked. No signs of coronary occlusion or myocardiac degeneration are to be found. He is discharged. Convalescence until July 30th is advised.

On his second discharge:

> He was admitted with precordial pains and paresthesias in face and body. His state is one of severe panic. At the hospital no signs of cardiac illness are to be found. If his attacks of panic continue, consultation with Dr. Vanggaard is advised.

On Sept. 8th of this year he again woke up during the night with feelings of panic, palpitations, and short-

[15]

ness of breath. There was no trace of precordial pressure or stinging, no dizziness or fear of madness. He was given a tranquilizing injection and felt low for most of the following day. He was taken to the hospital once more; the findings were again negative. Since then he has repeatedly had strong feelings of panic, both at night and during the daytime, coupled with fear of death, despite his knowledge that his condition is not dangerous. He had his last attack of panic of this kind the day before yesterday, which is why he came to me.

From here on his story will be told in the present tense as I recorded it, but mostly without quotes.

On the date given above—our first meeting—*A* told me that he has never been nervous before in his life; especially, he has had no similar attacks of panic, although he always had nightmares, by which he means dreams accompanied by panic, from which he awoke. He would be relieved as soon as he realized that it was only a dream, whereupon he would fall asleep again. As regards feelings of fear while awake, he said that he felt afraid once, earlier in his life in 1960, when he was managing a mission hospital in New Guinea where there were disturbances and many Europeans were being killed by the natives. The day before Christmas he had a message from the local police that a group of men from a neighboring village had plans to attack the hospital. Nothing came of it, however, since they drank to pluck up courage first, and apparently took too much. However, he spent that Christmas eve and night in mortal fear for himself, his wife, and his children. Nonetheless, he was outwardly calm. (This experience obviously has nothing to do with neurotic fear.)

Then he tells me that he has always had a tendency to become tense and impatient when his proposals for reform or improvement were not accepted quickly. During his stay in New Guinea he was regarded as a rather difficult person because of this. In a sense the same holds true here in Denmark, but he has no real difficulties cooperating with his colleagues. At the moment he feels a considerable tenseness and impatience, because reforms necessary for the instruction of students are not being implemented quickly enough. Under such circumstances, that is, when he is impatient, he may feel quite excited and his excitement may, for instance, make it difficult for him to sleep at night. He says, however, that he has no difficulties in communicating with others.

On being asked what his reaction is to hearing or reading about war, disasters, violence, torture, and the like, he immediately replies: "I can have nothing to do with such things; I have always avoided them entirely." He does not read about them in newspapers or books, very seldom goes to the cinema, and when a short time ago he accidentally heard a detailed description on the radio of a concentration camp and the grisly events which took place there, he felt so ill that he almost fainted. *

He is married to a woman somewhat younger than himself. He describes his marriage as happy. At the time of his first heart attack, when he believed that he had had a coronary thrombosis, his wife was frightened, but she has reacted to the subsequent ones with calm and composure. Conditions at work are good, he says: he is satisfied with his job. He could have obtained a professorship, but abstained from applying in favor of a colleague and friend of his own age, who, according to *A*

*These traits are typical elements of the character neurosis which forms the matrix of neurotic spells of panic.

[17]

himself, is a better scientist than he and has had poorer working conditions. His friend has just moved into the hospital as a professor. He describes his relationships to him and to professor N as the best conceivable. One more professorship will probably be created to which he will be appointed. An important additional reason for his not applying was the quantity of faculty work which goes with such a chair.

A is rather tall, an impressive man with an individual look to him, dark, with large features, polite and pleasant in his ways, obviously a strong, outgoing personality. But with this he betrayed also a certain sense of insecurity. He is intelligent, expresses himself well, has a sense of humor, and is most direct in his personal contact. He knows how to address an emotional appeal, but does so discreetly and tactfully.

September 19, 1969: The First Analytical Session

A lies on the couch. He speaks spontaneously and freely throughout the session. I sit behind him. He reports that he woke up last night, but had no real feeling of fear. However, some time after waking he had a sense of being at the hospital, and that the person lying beside him was a stranger. He has had similar experiences many times during his married life, especially during the first years, of feeling that the woman lying at his side was a total stranger. These have given him a deep sense of embarrassment.

He talks much about the difficulties of living in New Guinea, especially about the danger of his children catching illnesses.

September 22, 1969

Since *A* last left me, his thoughts have focused almost constantly on his stay in New Guinea. In 1965 he finally came home after seven years out there. He speaks with great and sincere feeling, at times on the brink of tears, of the difficulties he had at the mission hospital. He was brought up to worship missionaries and from his boyhood he had looked upon them as heroes. He had himself wanted to devote his life to this field. And it was like a personal satisfaction to his father when he went out to New Guinea. However, once out there, he was, from the very beginning, deeply disappointed at how bad the relationship was and how poor the cooperation between the missionaries. He also talks about the lack of understanding back home of conditions prevailing in a place like New Guinea. When one is home on leave one has to deliver some 50 speeches throughout the country on experiences "out there." But there are many topics which cannot be mentioned at all.

For example, it goes without saying that it is impossible to mention that the missionaries catch gonorrhea, or to allude to many of the conditions of native life. One example of this is an episode he has given much thought to since his last session. During a visit to a distant mountain village, where he went on house-to-house rounds together with leaders of the local congregation, he found, lying beside the road, a badly injured man, obviously the victim of a traffic accident. For one thing, he was in a state of advanced dehydration. He tried to make the local natives carry the man to the nearest dispensary, but they refused to do so. In spite of long parleyings, he finally had to give up and let the man lie where he was. Since then he has realized that such is the way of life there; you cannot demand of the population, on the basis of our values, that they should care for one another as we would do. Victims of a fight are treated in the same way; they are left where they are. The lot in store for them is often extremely unpleasant, as stray dogs start eating them before they are quite dead.

When on leave back home, at a small "drawing-room meeting," the first one held on his return, he told about the man he had to leave by the road, the first reaction was one of embarrassed silence; then someone present exclaimed: "In that case you are not the man we thought you were."

He goes on to speak of the many great difficulties he met in his work: of missionary doctors at the hospital who, because of their own mental imbalance, kept deserting the hospital, so that he might be without a surgeon for days on end; of the thieving and criminal habits of the native assistants—how, for instance, his first Indian assistant doctor got many of the native staff into his clutches by keeping them supplied with cocaine. In return they paid him their entire wages. His own servant, among others, did so. As time went by, this man became completely degenerate and in the end he was sentenced to gaol. It was also proved that this same assistant had the hospital's 20 native student nurses in his power to such an extent that he hired them out as prostitutes. In the evening, buses arrived and took the student nurses to the military brothel. The troubles caused by this were enormous. In the end he was able to back out of the whole thing by citing his children's need for a Danish school education.

A adds that that discovery of the goings-on at the nurses' home was particularly galling to him because there was one young girl whom he admired and of whom he thought highly. She proved to be implicated.

[20]

There were many problems with the families of these nurses. Pregnancy out of wedlock was a far greater calamity there than in Denmark.

He asks if these feelings which he has had over the last few days can mean that those bygone conflicts and problems are really the cause of his symptoms of panic. I answer that it can hardly be as simple as that. He tells me that he had a violent attack of panic a few days ago, but that he is now perfectly able to control himself and does not lose his head over it.

September 24, 1969

Again today he speaks in a lively and spontaneous way. He has had violent attacks of panic with intervals of three weeks. If the pattern continues, another one is due on Sunday. These attacks coincide with his wife's three weeks' menstrual cycle. She has mentioned the possibility of a connection herself. For some ten days before menstruation she has always been uninterested in sexual intercourse. Just after her period she is extremely interested and active, to the satisfaction of both of them. The regular monthly terms of abstinence have been a drag to him, "although to a lesser extent in later years." However, he has always regarded it as his duty to put up with them.

V: He should regard any attacks of panic not as something to be feared and avoided, but as something he must be prepared to incur from time to time and should look upon as an opportunity of training himself to endure and control fear. This *A* accepts.

Once again he speaks of conditions in New Guinea, of other aspects of missionary work. He paints—he did in New Guinea, too—allegorical pictures, as a rule. For instance, he painted a picture of a fat missionary with a large face and a greedy, cruel expression, devil's horns and ears, and a Bible in his hand, sitting in a rickshaw. He has apparently been interrupted in his reading by the fact that his emaciated coolie has dropped to the ground with blood gushing from his mouth. The picture contained several other details referring to the attitude towards the natives as lesser beings, as servants requiring guardianship in every way. This picture made quite a splash and elicited very conflicting reactions. Some people, even some missionaries, found that it truly reflected unfortunate aspects of the situation, which ought to be eliminated. Others were deeply offended by it. In the end he hid the picture. He has not been able to hang it in Denmark either, as it would seriously offend his father, were he to see it. "His whole world would go to pieces." He still thinks that what he expressed in this picture is right and true, but also that his view was one-sided, that the negative aspects of missionary work had come to blind him to all the others of his stay in New Guinea. What was done out there was, after all, not wholly bad.

He talks about his work in collaboration with Professor A. L. Hansen on cellular antigenes in autoimmunity defects. They seem to be on their way towards a truly effective treatment.

September 26, 1969

He starts by saying that he is a very happy and grateful patient. Since the day before yesterday he has been feeling "himself again."

V: I would say you ought not think of terminating the treatment on that account—just in case!

A: I have no intention of doing so.

He talks of the warm, close family relationship in his childhood home. He particularly remembers the festiveness of his whole family going to the Sunday School led by his father. Later on, when he reached puberty, his relationship to his parents took a turn for the worse, but it went back to normal when he reached adulthood.

He speaks at some length about his own engagement in the Boy Scout movement as a scoutmaster and about life in the resistance during the German occupation, when he was a member of a group receiving arms from the allied forces. He was notified that he was on a list of people to be killed. He went into hiding but did not escape to Sweden. He was not himself involved in killings.

September 29, 1969

He has had lesser attacks of panic, by day as well as by night, especially the night before last—the night between Saturday and Sunday, that is; but he had no difficulty in holding his panic off and making it subside. He had an extremely unpleasant *dream* last night: He was sitting for a viva voce examination in anatomy and had to explain a large cytological chart including coding of the formation of antibodies, cellular fission and so on, a symbolic account in mathematical terms of the many complex interrelations in the human organism. He could not cope. At the same time, he had an "absurd" but extremely painful feeling that, if he could not carry it off, the processes expressed in these equations could no longer function, but would stop; "I know it sounds silly, but in that case not only I myself, but humanity as such, would perish."

V: It is no "absurd" thought—on the contrary it is a thought common to man that he is responsible not only for his own destiny, but for that of the cosmos as a whole, and that he must maintain it by ritual and sacri-

fice. From the scientist's point of view this is meaningless, of course; but it is, nonetheless, a subjective reality
which cannot be eradicated by a mere scientific approach. His dream contains the additional irony that an
attitude to life, basic to mankind but rejected as unreal in
science, is cloaked in scientific material. (This comment
is an attempt to prepare him for the realization that,
deep down inside, he believes that his own emotions
and wishes affect the world and the people surrounding
him.)

A says that this makes a strong impression on him;
actually, many times in his life he has had a sudden sense
of being responsible for the true course of all things. He
felt troubled by it, and as well has always believed that
the assumption of such personal importance was an en-
croachment on the prerogative of the Almighty.

V: "This last statement is an expression of a restricted
view typical of modern Christianity. It is the consequence of a loss of the conviction, common to earlier
ages, that an ordered world results from a covenant between God and Man, depending on both for its maintenance."

A refers to several other occasions when he experienced
similar feelings of responsibility, even in his youth.

He talks at length of the sense of deprivation he has
felt at no longer being a member of a congregation.
Immediately after his return from abroad he was unable
to participate in parish life because, being still regarded
as a missionary, he would have been expected to speak
of "the work done out there." As indicated above, many
aspects of life in New Guinea could not be mentioned
because of a lack of understanding in Danish parochial
circles, and consequently, he preferred not to do so.
Living, as he does now, in a district where there is small
interest in church and parish matters, he longs for a
feeling of community such as he had known in the past.

October 1 and 3, 1969

He talks at length about the position of minority groups and the discrimination against them, using as an example the segregation in Denmark of schools into an A and a B stream, which he is much against, as he believes it to be morally wrong to separate pupils on grounds of ability: the inevitable result is that members of one group feel justified in looking down on those in the other, who receive a predominantly practical, as distinct from a scholarly, education. In the same vein he speaks of the problems facing colored people in both the United States and South Africa. He is all for equality, regardless of what it might cost the white population. In New Guinea where he had lived, there were, he reports, few whites, and he witnessed how they were harassed and intimidated to withdraw—he admits that the means employed were not very pleasant—for instance, pressuring their servants to leave them. He finds it a good thing, however, that the natives thus took over responsibility themselves. (It is evident throughout that he identifies with minority groups, indignantly and with much feeling; it would also appear that this may lead to conflict with his own group.)

Also, he talks about teaching at the university, which he considers inadequate for the students. His tone throughout is one of protest.

October 7, 1969

A has had a couple of minor attacks of panic, which he has kept well under control. "Now it is not so much a question of real panic; it is more of a sudden feeling of desolation. It is most illuminating to me to realize that I have been able to curb my own panic. I always believed such states should be treated with drugs."

[25]

Later in the session he says that birth control has become somewhat of a problem lately. Until recently he and his wife had wanted to have another child and have consequently not used any kind of birth control. However, his wife has not become pregnant and now, being 37, she believes she has grown too old and is no longer willing to risk it. She won't use a diaphragm, as she is prejudiced against it. Consequently he employs *coitus interruptus*. However, this entails a constant worry that the method might fail.

V: "*Coitus interruptus* is hardly a suitable method, especially for a man with a tendency to panic, since incomplete satisfaction promotes anxiety."

A feels that this method is satisfactory for him.

V: "Well and good, but what would you prefer, intercourse with or without interruption?"

A: "All right, you are correct in assuming that I would prefer it without interruption—on second thoughts, no, I wouldn't; because my wife feels sullied, when I have come inside her; it runs out again, you know."

(Here I let the matter rest, for the time being.)

October 8, 1969

A starts out at once telling me that what I said last session disturbed him somewhat. He has discussed it with his wife. Contrary to my suggestions about the importance of being sexually satisfied as fully as possible, he must claim, on reflection, that sexual satisfaction is probably of varying importance to different people. He realizes that to many it is crucial; but to him it has not been all that important. At school he had a crush on a girl or two, but distantly and very romantically. In his adult life he had no erotic interest in women for years, was never in love, and felt no physical need; he did not even flirt. When, as a student, he studied in the United States, he took no part in all the dating and petting which he saw going on so vigorously around him. Nor did he respond to the often quite aggressive advances from the girls. This was observed by those around him, and one teacher was concerned enough to say that it could not be good for his health to be so lacking in interest in girls. He ought to do something about it. During his years as a scoutmaster and in the resistance against the Germans he was completely absorbed in his work, and he never gave women a thought. As he grew older, although he felt no physical or emotional lack, he had from time to time a vaguely uneasy feeling that other people knew more about certain aspects of life than he did. When he began to masturbate after the onset of puberty, it was not, he claims, because of any powerful urge, but chiefly out of curiosity. During his adolescence and in his twenties he masturbated off and on and was not disturbed by guilt about it. For long periods he did not masturbate at all. He had nocturnal emissions now and then. On his own he adds that neither did he, in his many years among Boy Scouts, ever feel the least homosexual attraction.

He met his future wife, a nurse, while he was serving an obligatory graduate term. He liked her, and over the years they established a good personal relationship. She helped him in his scientific work. Working overtime, they were often alone together. Finally they got engaged. He proposed at a congress in Stockholm, to which she reluctantly accompanied him, despite the concern of her parents. When she had accepted him, she exclaimed: "Now you might give me a kiss!" Until then they had had no physical contact. Now, when he had to get on with it, he felt rather clumsy and awkward, but after a little while it went well. However, they continued to use the formal, polite Danish "you" to one another for some time after their engagement, but eventually they slipped into the familiar. (The two forms correspond to the French *vous* and *tu*.) With a laugh he adds: "Yes, I know it sounds funny." In answer to my explicit question he denies ever having had erections on bodily contect with her up to that point, and in spite of their kissing and fondling a couple of more months went by before he began to have erections. However, thereafter he began to be aroused and now he wanted her to have sex with him, but she did not want to before they were married. They both lived with their parents; there would have been practical difficulties. On their wedding night they did not have intercourse. He felt the situation awkward with, as it were, a strange woman in his bed; and she was nervous. So they contented themselves with some fondling; she was a virgin, after all. Some time passed—he does not remember how long—before they got around to it, but then they both became very eager. In this period they might have intercourse five times in a single night. At the time she declared herself fully satisfied, but he has since realized that this was not so. She experienced her first orgasm some three to four years later. Having an orgasm was a completely new experience for her, and she enjoys it very much. "But," he adds impulsively, "our general relationship has not at all been changed by it, it has always been good."

He concludes from all this that sexual satisfaction means less to him than to many other men, and thus that it does not make much difference whether he seeks a mode of intercourse that could give him a maximum of satisfaction or continues using *coitus interruptus*.

In any case, he states categorically, no other solution to the question of birth control is possible. His wife refuses to use a diaphragm; she is intensely reluctant to manipulate that part of her own body and she is against such a method of birth control, since, were she to become pregnant, she would accept it without protest even though throughout her pregnancies she had been sick and weary and depressed.

V: "Her attitude to birth control is self-contradictory, since you are allowed to practice *coitus interruptus*."

A: "True, I am well aware of that, but I am not bothered by paradoxes."

V: "Neither am I, necessarily; that is not my reason for stressing it. I only wish to call your attention to the fact that the revulsion felt by your wife against the use of a diaphragm must have another reason as well, namely, that she can avoid being "sullied" when you practice *coitus interruptus*." "Exactly," he answers.

(At the start of the session he had seen me searching in vain for a sheet of paper. He then said jokingly: "You had better find it, lest you run the risk of frustration." This is his way of making fun at my remark last session that *coitus interruptus* always involves a certain amount of frustration. As he leaves at the close of the session, he jokes again: "You had better find that page.")

October 10, 1969

A was affected by the last session. He has really been rather grumpy since. He does not believe I am right in assigning any importance to sexual frustration as a cause of his condition. He fully realizes that I have not claimed that this is the sole reason for it, but he does not think it plays any part at all. He also believes in the existence of other needs of equal or even greater importance than the sexual, such as a need to show consideration to other people. He is convinced that changing his wife's attitude towards using a diaphragm is out of the question. He is, himself, quite content with *coitus interruptus* and he regards the satisfaction of having considered her need as his own primary desire.

He is more inclined to believe that frustrations in his work may have a bearing on his condition. He has not managed to publish as much as he ought. During the spring he had twice rewritten a paper on some experimental work, at the request of Professor N, and it had been returned by the editor of the scientific journal with a set of critical remarks. Some about his style were justified; others were aimed at just the alterations he had made at the suggestion of N; and finally, there were quite unreasonable ones based on misunderstandings and incompetence. He has not yet been able to force himself to rewrite it once more.

After this he talks at length of his unsatisfactory teaching conditions, of the slow pace of change at the university, of his impatience at this, of whether or not he would want to be a professor under such circumstances and, on the other hand, of the frustrations in the long run if he were not one. In this connection he speaks with great respect of the colleague for whose benefit he withdrew voluntarily from the latest professorial appointment.

In this session, as in earlier ones, *A* exhibits a typical streak in his character: About his outer surroundings, especially with regard to institutional organization, he may be very discontent and impatient and complain freely. In close relationships, for example within his family or among those with whom he works intimately, he can bear no conflict; here everything must be peaceful, nice and comfortable.

October 13, 1969

It is now a couple of weeks since *A* has felt any real anxiety. During this time he has only felt downcast for short periods, as he did four days ago, and he believes this to be a substitute for his panic. During the weekend (today is Monday) he has been feeling very well. Yesterday he experienced a peace of mind which he does not recall feeling since he left for New Guinea. In consequence he thought he could do without his usual two light sleeping pills (meprobamate); however, he could not fall asleep and felt the onset of anxiety; he took to reading a book, whereupon he calmed down. Finally, at two o'clock, he took two of his sleeping pills and fell asleep.

The night before last he had a *dream* which was exceptional in that his wife figured in it. Normally he only dreams of his childhood or his work. He reports his dream thus: He was in bed with his wife. He wanted to have intercourse with her, but two disturbing factors prevented him. One was a swarm of tiny children crawling all over her as on Kay Nielsen's sculpture *The Water Mother* or *The Nile God*. The other was that his elder brother lay in another bed in the same room. "My elder brother, who was married many years before I was, actually provoked a terror of marriage in me. When I was still unmarried, his wife, from whom he is now divorced, wrote me a long letter in which she abused my brother vehemently and she actually wished him dead; on top of this she proposed that she and I start having an affair. In the future I took care not to be at home when my brother and she visited my parents, because she went for me, overtly and totally without shame. I believe I was by no means the only one.

"Something about my father served also, in some indefinable way, as a deterrent to marriage. I cannot explain what it was. I mean, he and my mother were happy together. My mother always talked about having children as something horrid. My wife never talked like that. She found it easy and actually looked forward to going to the maternity ward."

[31]

He goes on to speak about his wife and birth control. His own guess is that the many children in his dream expressed an apprehension on his part of his wife's becoming pregnant. She has recently stated that when she reaches the age of 40—that is to say, in two years—she no longer wants to risk pregnancy. At that time she would like to practice some kind of birth control, and he believes that she is thinking, more specifically, of an IUD so that she would not have to manipulate her own genitals.

V: "In that case, do you think she would tolerate your sullying her with your emission, or would she still demand that you withdraw?"

A replies that he does not know, but he would imagine that she might be willing to put up with it without objections just as she did when she intended to get pregnant. Incidentally, he thinks it quite possible that by talking about it she is indicating that she might be becoming gradually more willing to use birth control in the near future.

Right now their sex life is good. She has entered a phase of lively interest in sex; actually hers is greater than his. He finds daily intercourse rather more than he would want if it were up to him.

V: "Do you have difficulties in keeping up with it?"

A: "No. I am able to perform when it is expected of me. Perhaps age has dulled my appetite somewhat?"

V: "I don't think it is a question of age. I believe that your sexuality is trammeled in certain ways which lie beyond your own control. This was dominant in your youth, when you felt no erotic urge at all. After your marriage your reluctance towards sexual gratification gradually subsided, but I presume that it is still present to some extent. I believe that your dream demonstrates a factor in your mental life which may be one cause of

[32]

your holding back, viz. the presence of a prohibitive male figure which inhibits your wish for intercourse. In this case it is your elder brother, who once actually played such a part. When you so obligingly balked at your sister-in-law's advances, your antipathy towards her can hardly have been your only reason; the fact that your brother stood between you must have contributed to your course of action." He accepts this without hesitation.

V: "The forbidding figure might also be your father of whom you just spoke."

A also accepts this.

October 15, 1969

At once *A* says: "Your remark about my father last session got us to the core of the matter. I have actually been wrestling with his shadow since last I left you." *A* goes on to speak of his very ambivalent relationship to his father. He is very like him, in stature as well as voice, gait, and gestures. At home his father always acted as a strong and dominating person, very much the patriarch of the family. Especially as a child, before puberty, *A* was happy with his father, not least at Sunday School, but also when his father told the children stories—he was good at it. At the onset of puberty, however, his father changed his attitude toward the boys. Before, he would take them on his knee and be loving towards them; when they reached puberty he changed completely. He might then display a positive disgust at the changes in the boys' bodies. He would stop in front of *A*, look at him critically and with loathing, and say: "Look at all your pimples; but then, that's because you are at the awkward age." *A* claims that what rubbed his father the wrong way were clearly the bodily changes of adolescence as such.

[33]

On top of this came his father's religious attitude, a twisted version of a strict Evangelical branch of Danish Lutheranism. He dressed his whole world in shrouds. Everything was sinful. As a boy, A never went to the cinema, the theater, a ball, or the like—that was not allowed. Anything of a sexual nature met with his father's stern disapproval. One of A's elder brothers moved out of the home in protest, took a room in town, and formed a liaison with a girl friend, who is now his wife. She got pregnant and had an illegal abortion, mostly because A's brother did not dare to tell his parents about the pregnancy. However, she fell ill as a result of the abortion and was confined to bed for some time at the house of A's parents. His mother treated her rather harshly, and the situation was not pleasant. It is his father's express attitude that birth control is not permissible. Hence the seven children. However, at the same time he would complain about having so many children.

Since he was a child, A has been afraid of his father and seen him in a sinister light. For instance, his father would always take care of the furnace, and A sees him clearly shoveling coal into it with the red glow falling on his face. It looked frightening. When he was a boy he often had alarming dreams involving his father. He remembers one very unpleasant dream vividly: He was to be burnt but asked those who were to do it to burn his father and eldest brother instead. They actually did so, set fire to them, and they went off like firecrackers. It was very frightening.

When he realized that he was in love with the woman to whom he is now married, he told his mother, and she passed it on to his father. It did not go down well with them, and for a while the atmosphere was charged and unpleasant. In an attempt to alleviate this, he invited her home to dinner one evening. With her excellent ability to hit it off well with other people, she succeeded in establishing a good rapport with his father, who thawed completely, had fun, and told stories. When *A* had taken her to the bus and returned, his father said: "I think you should marry that girl." Although this was, of course, very gratifying, deep down he was annoyed and was on the brink of retorting that, after all, he and not his father was the one who would be marrying her. This was typical of the way in which his father always wanted to dominate.

When *A* and his wife returned from New Guinea, they both had a strong impression that somehow his father intended to make sure that they did not have any more children, as he did not think they could afford it.

His eldest brother always took his father's side and, during their childhood, he was the one who always squealed to him, the family spy. (This was the brother in last session's dream.)

"Well, I could go on like this for a long time, recounting episodes about my father. My mother was subservient to him in all things. I myself can get very annoyed when I visit them. For instance, papa will insist on having their white curtains drawn so the sun cannot shine on his furniture, even though their big lovely house has a splendid view of the Sound. They are like shrouds."

October 17, 1969

A begins by saying that he has felt much panic since last session. Later the same day, when he gave a lecture together with a colleague, who was to speak first, his colleague spoke for a long time, approximately an hour. While listening to him, *A* got into such a panic that he had to leave the lecture hall for 10 minutes. Afterwards he spoke his own piece without trouble.

I seriously enjoin him not to give in to his panic in this way.

A says that he has had many attacks ever since. He woke up in panic last night and while he sat here waiting for me this morning he also felt anxious in anticipation. This anxiety, however, lacks the previous deeply disturbing heart symptoms. He himself believes that it is caused by talking of his father in the way he did last session.

V: "From a therapeutic point of view it is a good sign that your reaction was one of panic, as this shows the presence of important conflict matter."

A tells me that while he lay last night feeling afraid, an early childhood memory came to mind. He does not know whether it was a dream or whether it actually happened: A large butchered turkey or hen was lying on the kitchen table and cook had dressed it in his youngest brother's clothes. It was very uncanny.

He returns to talking of his father—he wants a good relationship with him, after all.

For the rest of the session I speak to him about his inner tensions and conflicts. On the one hand he is eager for reform, quick to be indignant and critical in a way which is often clamorous, impatient, and maladroit, inasmuch as he does not manage to adapt well to the situation at hand, however right he might be about the facts. This applies in particular to authorities, institutional leaders, and the like. On this account he has often been labeled combative and impetuous. On the other hand, in intimate circles, such as his family or among close colleagues at the department, he wants absolute peace and quiet. Actually it is only with difficulty that he is able to acknowledge the existence of conflict in these spheres. He has thus split his world in two, so that he is almost overaggressive within one part of it and intentionally unaggressive in the other. At the same time, his family situation is clearly tense. He feels enmity, anger, annoy-ance towards his father, even if, as a rule, he does not show it to his face and would prefer to have a tranquil relationship with him.

On the whole it is more probable that his childhood recollection was a dream, and in that case the slaughter of his brother took place in his own fantasy. Should it have been cook's idea, however, it could only have made such an impression on him by appealing to feelings and fanta-sies of his own. "True," he replies, "especially when one remembers it so vividly after the lapse of 40 years."

During this session he has spoken of meetings at the hospital, of future planning to be undertaken, and of laying down a new curriculum. In this connection there is talk of setting up a new department, "and of course they are looking to me as the coming professor to take charge of it." This makes him uneasy, as he does not at all know if he would manage such a task, seeing how nervous he may still become, as witness his recent expe-rience at the lecture.

V: "You must regard this unease at accepting a chair which would fall to you in the natural course of events as a neurotic symptom and treat it accordingly. You must not give in to your unease, nor let it influence your decision with regard to reality. It is my considered opin-ion that your withdrawal in favor of P should also be regarded as a neurotic symptom which you exhibited before your neurosis became manifest, despite the good moral reasons you gave for doing so. That is to say, it was the result of those character traits of yours which also form the basis of your neurosis. Among other things, they reveal themselves in the conflict you feel between a strong ambition and an equally strong apprehension at accepting those high posts to which you aspire." "Yes, that is true," he laughs.

[37]

At one point I mentioned that this tension is closely connected with his relationship to his father and that it was developed and accentuated in that relationship.

During the session he remarked that his attitude towards his stay in New Guinea has straightened itself out. He no longer feels uncomfortable about it and is able to talk in a relaxed way about it to everybody. Now he could also lecture on it without a qualm.

October 22, 1969

A visited his father last weekend. His father sat indoors despite the brilliant sunshine, with white linen curtains drawn and sheets over the furniture to protect the upholstery. "He is eccentric, you know." Then he continues: "The color of the curtains, a yellowish white, makes me very uncomfortable, probably because I associate it with a dream I had as a child: In a cellar, some large rubber bottles containing a white liquid stood along the walls. The white stuff consisted of dissolved human beings, and the containers were shaped like ear syringes so the contents could be squirted out of them." He had this dream at a time when the head of the Sunday School was constantly telling his pupils that they should get used to the idea of dying, of how you grow cold, how your blood coagulates, and your breathing stops. For A death has always been associated with mental pictures of strangulation, hanging, and decapitation. In India he saw many people die, many of tubercular dyspnea.

His own conception of afterlife would be experiencing a close togetherness with kin and friends, an experience of a kind which, in this life, we may know in part during intercourse or efficient teamwork, or something like that. This experience, he adds, is much more common to non-Europeans than to us. It is a natural by-product of their everyday lives. The difference between them and us also shows in their patterns of thought. They have a specific idiom for the way white men think, for which we have no equivalent. But what it actually means is that to them our way of thinking is always to look for a single connection or cause, while they as a matter of course always reckon wih multiple connections and causes, weighing one against another. This pattern of thought is part and parcel of their communal life and their way of settling matters in cooperation. This is the communal spirit, so foreign to us, in which a single member of the community does not primarily consider his own contributions and advantages. He came to know it intimately from men still rooted in tribal society, such as a friend of his who is now, to the indignation of the whites, chief administrator of the hospital in New Guinea. Natives who are removed from the tribal community to which they belong and receive a "white" education lose contact with it to a large extent, and the worst scoundrels among them—such as the assistant doctor mentioned earlier—are the direct result of the work of the missionary societies. That is because of the misconception prevailing among white men that if you take a native and put him in at one end of a white educational system he will come out at the other as an excellent character. Very often what happens is exactly the reverse, because he is detribalized and, as a result, loses something of value which we do not possess.

October 24, 1969

To begin with, *A* tells me about his mother-in-law's birthday party a few days ago, of the warm atmosphere among her friends, who have faithfully stuck together since their childhood, and of their warm and fun-loving conversation. His own family's rather rigid parties are very different: formal, boring, and as often as not sarcastic.

He goes on to tell me that the experiments he is conducting in the department of Professor A. L. Hansen do not seem to be proceeding according to plan. He stops talking, puts his hand to his brow; then he says: "How strange, I suddenly feel ill."

V: "What is the matter?"

A: "My heart is giving me trouble, and I feel panicky." Shortly afterwards he says: "Well, it's passed, but now I just feel empty. I don't know what to say. I don't understand; I don't usually have trouble finding something to say to fill in a break."

V: "I believe your attack is due to repressed tension in relation to me. Your feelings towards nearly everyone else are ambivalent. It seems almost unthinkable that you should not harbor similar feelings towards me. I suggest that you are trying to divest our relationship of this tension, just as you do in relations to those close to you, members of the family, colleagues."

A: "That is true."

V: "Undoubtedly you will try to do same with me."

A: "That is true."

V: "I cannot imagine that your relationship to me can be entirely free of elements that might disturb the safe and tranquil relationship you prefer. Anything of the kind would probably crop up to make you tongue-tied, and you would pause in your narrative. However, as you say yourself, usually you cover up by inventing something to fill in with.

A (after a slight hesitation): "Yes, it is true, of late I have been trying to keep my religious view of life out of my communications with you. I have the feeling that, after all, I have to have something I can call my own and I am afraid of being in some way influenced by you in

[40]

this matter." He is aware, he explains, that by coming here he has already changed his views on many subjects and he would rather avoid any such change in his religious convictions.

V: While replying that this is quite understandable, and that he need not fear any direct attempt on my part to influence him in this respect, I also explain to him that his reasoning is a cover-up for a much more general fear of losing his independence to me, of succumbing to my influence. Such fear, I make clear to him, is common in a situation such as this in which he has of his own will accepted a dependency on me, and a degree of openness he would never have shown anyone, were it not for the burden of his symptoms. As a consequence he is afraid of losing his integrity, and this is the most likely background for the attack of fear he experienced a short while ago. However, such direct reactions towards me will mirror similar relationships in his life as a whole, and working on this may be very rewarding. I would therefore encourage him to tell me what he thinks of me, what his relationship is towards me, what his opinion of me is with the same unqualified frankness he has displayed in respect to so many other matters that he does not discuss with other people.

A: "Well, it won't be easy; but I see what you mean."

October 27, 1969

A immediately says that he has had a terrible time since last session. In the middle of a meeting he had with Professors N and P he had an attack of panic, his heart throbbed so violently the instruments he carried in the breast pocket of his white coat started rattling. However, he controlled himself so that they did not notice anything, and then it passed.

On his way home from the hospital that afternoon he

took to considering and assessing what it was he really believed in. And then nothing was left to him. Only, as it were, a great yawning abyss. It is the most terrible experience he has ever had, because this feeling of being in an abysmal void persisted. It suddenly became clear to him that this was exactly how he had felt when he had his first attacks of panic and was taken to the hospital. But at that time he did not realize—as he does now— that the cause of his panic was his religious doubt and his fear of the sense of abysmal desolation he gets from acknowledging that doubt. The sense of desolation and fear which he feels is exactly that expressed in Munch's painting, "The Scream." In the end, it is this sense of desolation and the dread of it which Munch is constantly depicting, representing it by the loneliness which can arise between people who have lost their sense of togetherness, as with the kinsfolk gathered around the deathbed of Munch's sister, all standing with faces averted from one another, alone and with nothing to say to each other. The ivory white of the face of the woman in "The Scream" is the color he spoke of in the next-to-last session, which he found so disgusting and abhorrent.

He has never before been willing to acknowledge in himself the religious doubts of which he has now become conscious. But he realizes they have existed for a long time, at least since his arrival in New Guinea, and that is at least ten years ago. "But the strange thing is that I am only able to perceive them now, at the age of 44."

During the day following his sleepness night he was gradually able to get back some fragments of his former convictions, mostly by reading hymns by Grundtvig, who, among others, as he now realizes, had to wrestle with the same kind of doubts and fears of desolation as he feels now. It must be a fear similar to the one expressed by Jesus on the cross: "My God, my God, why hast thou forsaken me?"

V: Tillich, the great American divine, expressly claims
that a basic condition of human existence is that Man
finds himself standing on the brink of a yawning chasm:
It is, he claims, an inescapable essential which Man may
either deny—as *A* did earlier; or he may endure by making it the cornerstone of his existence—as Munch did; or
he may face it and, accepting it, find a way to live
through it.

A: "Yes, I can see the last solution is the only viable
one."

Having had his eyes opened to this feeling of desolation, he was able to control his fear, despite the deep
unease and anxiety it caused him. He did not even feel
any urge to wake up his wife to tell her about it during
his sleepless night.

October 29, 1969

A begins by explaining that he has been feeling well but
experienced a strange repugnance towards coming here
today. He had the same feeling yesterday. Could it be
because he has had to go through rather unpleasant experiences while he was here, and yet had to keep
coming, or is it because he is now so much better that he
no longer feels such an urgent need to come to me as
before?

V: "Both. The unpleasantness which treatment involves inevitably creates a resistance against such expo-
sure of oneself; and, feeling better, you are tempted not
to regard treatment as such a necessity anymore."

For the rest of the session he talks of the future curriculum and about how inconvenient it is that the hospital
buildings are being converted, what with people ham-
mering, fussing around, laying cables, and so on. He is
clearly filling out a long pause, an obvious device of
resistance. However, I avoid interfering with it, partly

[43]

because I think he should be given a breather; moreover, I have to cancel the following two sessions and I do not want to risk starting up something which I cannot follow through during the next days.

We arrange for him to come again after a week.

A: "Good, I am doing so well now that I can easily manage."

November 5, 1969

A comes back after skipping two sessions because of my cancellation. He starts by saying that he enjoyed this little vacation: "You shouldn't misinterpret that! But it was nice to put you and all this at a distance." One night four days ago, when he lay awake with feelings of fear, a lot of memories of his mother's bedroom came up. He had not thought of these things for 20 years. In his childhood his family lived in a house in Hellerup, a wealthy suburb of Copenhagen. His parents' bedroom was on the first floor; it had brown walls, a white ceiling, two large double beds painted brown, and a large old-fashioned wardrobe. To *A* this was always a special room: One came there in the morning on one's birthday and got one's present; one also came to get spanked there—that would happen from time to time. It was also the room where his mother gave birth to his four younger brothers and sisters, and he remembers the midwife coming with her paraphernalia and some yellowish white rubber sheets for his mother to lie on. It was all rather uncanny. From time to time the children were allowed into the bedroom with their father, who usually got up a little later than their mother, and who would then tell them stories. Once he also tried to tell him about human reproduction, but that rather misfired. He was pompous and bungled it, finally managing to say something to the effect that there was something which went from the father into the mother, and that it came out of his penis. However, this explanation left A with the impression that the father peed into a glass, and the mother then drank it. At any rate this was what he believed for a long time afterwards.

The matter of his professorship now seems to be shaping up. Premises can be made available at the hospital. He is now all for the project, which he was previously against on the pretext that he did not want to leave the other two departments. However, he has now swung round "and that's thanks to you, because in fact I was scared of being independent and shouldering the responsibility, and now I realize that was a symptom I should fight."

November 7, 1969

A felt somewhat afraid the day before yesterday; however, "not nearly as much as before." He had experienced some trifling vexations that day, among other things an encounter with a young colleague. That afternoon he felt annoyed for much longer than he himself found reasonable. For the rest of the day he felt tense and was afraid; then during the night he had "a strange dream in which you figure." The *dream:* I was conducting a kind of medical examination of A's wife. It included sticking hypodermic needles into her, which she found unpleasant, and at one point cutting open her drawers. She was very much against this, but I insisted, and she had to put up with it. I then had demanded to see whether or not their genitals were on a level when they were standing up. He expostulated, knowing that there was a difference of three inches. ("In fact I don't know anything of the sort.") Moreover, he tried to plead that this was obvi-

[45]

ously irrelevant while lying down, but again I insisted.

He then says: "After this dream all my feelings of fear were gone—interesting, isn't it? For this dream obviously bears on matters we have discussed."

V: "How is that?"

A: "You see, even though I am aware of the fact that you said from the start these were matters I had to decide myself, I have felt all along that if my wife's attitude—towards birth control and *coitus interruptus*, you know—has a bearing on my condition, I should have to tackle the question. I *have* asked my wife if we could reconsider the matter. She answered that in that case she would have to have one of those IUD's inserted. However, she then grew taciturn and depressed, and we lost all rapport. Some time after arriving at the hospital I rang home and told her not to give it any further thought. Since then blissful relations have been reestablished. Just now is a period in which she is very active sexually. We have wonderful relations, and truly I don't attach any importance to that question of *coitus interruptus*."

V: "Yes, the dream is transparent." I say that it also shows how he has felt cornered by me in this matter; he is disturbed by the feeling that I want to decide about him and his conjugal relations and to pressure him to comply with my decisions. He has also been worried by fears of a possible clash with me, were he not willing to take my advice.

A: "True." Rationally he is of course well aware that I have taken pains to deny any such interpretation, but he admits to the existence of another—complementary—attitude.

V: "Yes, and that is the one loaded with emotion."

A: "Yes."

V: "It is a general trait of yours that you have difficulty tolerating conflicts. They call forth emotions which vex you for a long time, as in the case of your young colleague."

A (before I have alluded to his wife): "The day before yesterday, in connection with my feeling of fear, I suddenly felt totally different than I usually do towards my wife. She suddenly seemed to be no fun, I didn't even really like her, and I have never felt like that before; on the contrary we are so happy together."

He goes on spontaneously: They only once had a really blazing row. It was some years ago—to the best of his memory it was because he demanded that dinner should be served on the dot; otherwise he would have hypoglycemia attacks. "Imagine the abuses science must take the blame for," he comments with a grin. He adds that he clashed with his wife just before he had his initial attack of panic and was taken to the hospital. They had hired a young musician to teach both of them. The man strongly criticized the way his wife played, while praising A's playing highly. On top of this the fellow was one of those long-haired types which neither of them likes. A's wife took an intense dislike to him. This caused strong feeling between them, "and I actually believe that this was the immediate cause of my attack of panic."

V: "It is probably an important observation that tension in your relationship to your wife contributes strongly to your panic."

This ends the session.

November 10, 1969

To begin with A tells me that he has reduced his dose of sleeping medicine to one tablet of meprobamate; he sleeps well on that. He has realized, he goes on, that he has actually had several serious conflicts with his wife during their marriage—"I just didn't want to admit it to

[47]

myself''—and they were chiefly of a sexual nature. "For one thing my wife doesn't want intercourse during the last ten days before her period, as I have mentioned. She shows an interest out of consideration for me, but she holds aloof. But another thing is that she finds it difficult to obtain release, and when she does, it takes a long time." (*A* mentions this to me for the first time.) "I have often been bitter about it. Just before I had my first massive attack of panic, which was when she was adverse to intercourse, I had urged her on, but she couldn't cooperate at all, and therefore I interrupted the proceedings, giving as my reason that it was a shame to put her through it when she disliked it. This was not the true reason by any means; I was angry with her, and withdrawing was simple revenge so that she could lie and "stew in her own juice." (He uses the English idiom; Danish has none so crudely apt.) "And the reason I gave didn't even give her a decent chance to voice any dissatisfaction."

"She has got over that now, I believe. She is in her active phase at the moment, and everything is just fine between us." (I deliberately refrain from asking him if, despite her sprightliness, she is still tiresomely slow to reach orgasm.)

He goes on to tell me of other serious conflicts between them. After they were married she was homesick for a while, and he felt that she regretted her marriage, but he never discussed it with her. Later, when he wanted to go to New Guinea, she was strongly against their going. He was finally so fed up with her resistance that he declared that, considering her attitude, he would not leave under any circumstances, although actually the whole thing was as good as settled. "And, after all, that was the same thing as with the recent intercourse. It was

[48]

revenge: If that was her attitude, she could have her pleasure and be welcome to it." Thus pressured she was not willing to take the responsibility of staying in Denmark and gave in entirely. Once out there, she adapted well, much better than he did.

They had a crisis in their sexual life while in New Guinea: He was impotent for a while. That was before she had ever had an orgasm. Although at the time he suffered from malaria and had had quite a rumpus with the missionary leaders, he thinks that his bitterness at her inadequacy contributed to his impotence.

With respect to birth control he still believes that it is imperative to wait for a couple of years, when she might want to have an IUD, "but I don't think this detail is at all important."

His eldest brother paid him a visit; they had a pleasant evening which made him happy. He alludes once more to this brother's wife. In the letter in which she propositioned him she also suggested that the two of them together should murder his brother. Thereafter he refused to be at home when she and his brother visited their parents, who found this so remarkable that they urgently demanded to know why, brushing aside his lame attempts to explain away the facts. In the end he showed them the letter. His mother took it and gave it back to his sister-in-law, who, by the way, has since been admitted as a patient to a psychiatric department somewhere, so far as he knows. This summer, just before he had his first attack of panic, he caught sight of her at the hospital. He thought she had come to get her claws into him; it turned out, however, that she had come to do some secretarial work for one of his colleagues.

A has visited his father, and it went well. "I believe I can tackle him much easier now, since I acutely feel that

[49]

his problems are similar to mine. He always wants every-thing to be straightforward and without contradictions; and he hasn't got a Vanggaard to help him sort it out."

Leaving, he asked: "Do you still think it necessary that I come here and bother you?"

V: Yes, I do.

(This last remark is, of course, a patent show of resis-tance, and his avowals of how well he is, although by no means unsubstantiated, should also be seen as resis-tance.)

November 12, 1969

For almost the entire session *A* keeps to neutral subjects, conditions at the hospital and the like. I get a clear im-pression that he is "filling in a long pause" as he once called it. However, finally he says: "After our talk last time I have had uneasy thoughts, a kind of anxious feel-ing that I might be heading for a showdown with my wife. I have realized that I have problems with my mar-riage, after all, which I have refused to acknowledge until now—this is what you so nicely call 'a deeper in-sight into one's own mind.' I'm scared that this may mean our marriage is on the rocks. When I think of what has emerged as a result of my coming here, I cannot help feeling anxious about what the future may hold."

A's next remarks reveal that his anxiety is paradoxical: He is afraid lest his wife should suddenly review their marriage and reject it as impossible.

I stress that his question at the end of last session—about whether his continued treatment was becoming a nuisance to me—was an expression partly of his evident fear of the risks involved, partly of his desire to steer clear of those risks. This, with a laugh, he admits. I go on to suggest that when he feels deeply threatened by

his discontent with his married life, by his wrath towards his wife and his desire to take revenge, he seeks
to ward off the danger. He does this by dissociating himself from feelings and attributing them to his wife, so
that in his imagination it is she who wants a divorce although, as things stand, nothing points in that direction. He admits the truth of this. He ponders it and understands.

While discussing this I said that I believed he was
quite obviously afraid that I was going to try to force
him into angry, vengeful showdowns with his wife, possible even into divorcing her. He frankly admits that he
has been afraid of just that. In passing I add that naturally nothing is further from my intention than to disturb
his marriage, but that I am bound to think it very unwise
should he abandon treatment out of fear of the risks
involved. "Touché," he replies.

November 14, 1969

A starts by saying that he has given much thought to our
conversation during the last session. There are certain
things he cannot quite make out, "but maybe it isn't all
that important." He then talks about the gist of the last
session, his unfounded fear that his wife would want a
divorce "or possibly start a big row, which I would also
find extremely unpleasant, as you know." He comments
on my remarks in this connection, particularly that I
claimed that he had attributed his own emotions to her.
(He speaks of this in a somewhat perplexed and mud-
dled way, typical of patients who, because of emotional
involvement in some matter, are unable to master it.)

I sum up the situation and so indicate that obviously
he does not make a clear distinction between (1) acknowledging his angry, hurt feelings (like those he har-

[51]

bors about his wife's sexual inhibitions), and thus being able to see them as they are, and assess and control them; and (2) giving in to such feelings in outward action. He tends to believe that emotion leads directly to action, which is why he has been so much afraid to admit the existence of his angry dissatisfaction with his wife that he has denied and suppressed it with a vengeance. But the net result is that those angry, dammed-up feelings will *either* erupt at the slightest provocation—as they did in the blow-up he had with his wife some years ago about dinner (*A* reverted to this episode earlier this session)—*or* they will result in attacks of panic. *For his panic is in fact a reaction to his own suppressed feelings of hatred*.

A becomes very thoughtful at this. Apparently he feels things fall into place; he says as much and concludes that the right thing to do must be what he never dared before: that is, admit the reality of his obviously conflicting emotions towards his wife. "But this is contrary to all our previous resolutions since we have always agreed to be completely frank and mutually trustful, and never have thoughts about one another we were not willing to share."

V: "This is a fatal attitude in marriage; it can only result in a refusal to face facts and their consequent repression." *A* nods his thoughtful assent and gives as parallel the mania for confession he has encountered in some religious sects where people are wont to seek out each other saying: "I confess to the sin of being angry with you because of so and so"—actually submitting the other person to venomous reproach.

He recalls a sharp attack of panic many years ago when he was 26. This attack was identical to the one which led to his hospitalization. While on a photo safari

[52]

in Kenya he was cut off from the others because he stayed a little too long on an island where they were taking pictures of hippopotamus. The river unexpectedly rose around the island and he had to stay there in the black of a tropical night. From the river he could hear the rutting hippos roar as they fought one another. By dusk several of them came up onto the island to browse. He had a violent attack of panic accompanied by a hail of ectopic heartbeats. It was all quite horrible and did not stop until the following day, when the water level dropped and he was able to join his fellows. Up to now he had believed the actual cause of his panic to be the hippos and the dark. But he would now say only that they triggered it. In reality hippos are only dangerous if you threaten their young, although they can then indeed be mortally dangerous. He knew that he had nothing to fear if only he kept quiet.

He then says: "Well, what do you think could be the reason for that attack of panic?"

V: "After the lapse of so many years I do not think there's an easy answer."

A: "On the contrary, there is." Not long before, he had been living with a group of students, the rest of them quite openly engaged in *la dolce vita*, something he did not want any part of, as already mentioned. But it actually piqued him and he ran away from it to Kenya. His own opinion now is that the hippos triggered a dammed-up tension caused by his stay with the student group. With a smile he adds: "It must be boring for you to watch how laboriously I inch my way towards conclusions you probably reached ages ago."

I explain to him that, on the contrary, it is very satisfying to the therapist to watch such labor, whereby the patient, by his own efforts, achieves insight.

[53]

November 17, 1969

The night before last *A* did not sleep well. He felt no actual panic but slept fitfully, constantly waking up, and he had unpleasant *dreams*, one of which he remembers: Someone—"I am not quite sure who it was; it may have been you or my wife or my father"—wanted to make him walk down a newly made road near his home, "and it was very unpleasant." Later he dreamt "an odd and distasteful dream": He was beating up his son with his fists, violently and brutally. "Following your earlier interpretations of such dreams, I must acknowledge that my dream is in some way a true reflection of myself. I find this hard to believe especially about this boy—prepubertal and, as so often is the case with boys of his age, presenting no problems at all: He is a good boy in every respect, does well at school, and is even at the top of his class."

I am just about to remark that his boy may be a cover-up for other persons, but before the words are out of my mouth, he goes on to say: "But maybe I should not focus too much on the fact that he is the person I treat this way in my dream. While pondering over it yesterday I suddenly realized how typical it is of me that I always and immediately establish an emotional relationship with people with whom I come in touch. A student who seeks me out with a problem is instantly either a poor, insecure youngster who needs compassion and a maximum of support, or a tiresome fellow who came to annoy me on purpose. Oddly enough, come to think of it, I attended a youth service yesterday. The church was full to the last seat, we were packed in like sardines. We were late because we had walked through the Royal Deer Park. We ran into some red stags fighting in the middle of the footpath, so we had to make a detour. The youngsters who sang at the service were the kind with long hair and sunglasses. But they sang well just the same. Jammed up against me was a man whom I felt I ought to know, but for the moment I couldn't place him. This strangely excited me and set my heart to throbbing, but I wasn't actually afraid. Only afterwards did I realize that he was a student whom I had flunked for the third time. He had been studying for years on end and has a wife and kids; but he was just no good.

"Although, strictly speaking, I find it hard to accept, I have to admit that in my relations with other people I am governed by such extreme emotions and that I may even harbor entirely contradictory feelings towards one and the same person, especially if it is a person very close to me. In that case I usually just shelve all my disagreeable and embarrassing feelings while bringing out the positive ones and playing them up." He continues talking about this with apparently a very clear and profound insight into his relations with, for example, his wife and close colleagues. He adds that just now he probably tends to exaggerate the importance of his hostile feelings in these otherwise good relationships.

I hasten to assure him that in the majority of relationships positive emotions are not negated by the insight that they do not reign supreme. However, he has, undoubtedly, often been forced to inflate the positive feelings in order to hide the hostile and rancorous ones from himself. I follow this up by discussing in some detail the unrealistic nature of a relationship which results from insisting on one or the other of the two extremes of emotions simultaneously felt. This certainly holds true if, as an additional consequence, one has difficulties in establishing unemotional, matter-of-fact relationships towards, say, the students one examines.

[55]

He quite realizes the price he has had to pay for this and also that repression of antagonistic feelings may result in attacks of panic. Pensively he adds: "I am, of course, vitally involved in all this; but at the same time it is a matter of great intellectual interest to me to observe so many aspects of myself of which I had no prior knowledge."

November 19, 1969

Since last session *A* has felt moderate anxiety, but only at night, not during the daytime. Especially, he was unable to sleep for a long time last night because of moderate anxiety. When he finally began to seek a possible reason he realized that he was sexually aroused. When this became clear, he fell asleep, "but of course I wouldn't know whether it was *post* or *propter*." In response to my query he confirms that she is now in her premenstrual period when she is averse to intercourse.

He reverts to the subject of his tendency to establish emotional relationships, even with people who do not give him the slightest grounds for doing so. It is now clear to him how ingrained this tendency is. When traveling on the local train, for instance, he cannot keep the people around him from touching him emotionally, in either a friendly or a hostile way, though not a word passes between them.

Later in the session he says there is one thing he must discuss with me, which is that he is becoming increasingly uneasy that in the long run he will not be able to conceal the fact that he comes here for treatment. Today he ran into Professor N at the station, who naturally would not be able to understand what was keeping him from coming straight to the hospital. He is apprehensive particularly since soon he will be applying for the professorship himself. "But I realize that I am not the best judge of when I should stop coming. Last time, when I thought it wasn't necessary any longer, it was obviously premature; so I have decided to keep on coming, and gratefully too, for as long as you think necessary."

V: "Marked symptomatic improvement is always a turning point, and may create a resistance against continuing treatment." My considered opinion, however, is the same as before: Even though he can now, undoubtedly, manage without any symptoms worth mentioning, it would still be unwise of him not to derive whatever profit he can from continued treatment.

A replies that, oh yes, he quite agrees with me. He only wants to know how to handle the matter with regard to his colleagues. His own conclusion is that if N or P asks any questions about what he has been doing when he is late, or if the subject is brought up in any other way, he is going to say that he consults me to make sure that there are no signs of relapse from his "overworked state" last summer.

November 24, 1969

A starts by saying that he clearly understands that it would be too early to terminate his treatment. The other night he had a horrid dream; in fact, he never remembers having a worse one. It proves to him beyond doubt that he has many aspects which still need working over.

The *dream:* He was being examined and was expected to solve one of the large equations stating the cytological correlations in the human body (of which he dreamt once before). His wife was present as one of the examiners. This time he would himself die if he could not solve the equation. It was terrible. However, in the end he found a solution; he isn't quite sure what it was, but he woke up in a euphoric state, which was unsavory and uncanny: This euphoria somehow consisted of a malicious gloating at everybody else. Although he cannot remember in detail what the solution was, his notion is that it consisted of his actually giving up, thus committing suicide. "Serve them right" was the meaning of his gloating. This disturbing and unpleasant euphoria lasted all morning until he went to church, where he received Holy Communion and heard two stanzas of Grundtvig's hymn, well-known in Denmark, "The Land of the Living":

O Charity true,
Still Fount of the Torrent of Forces,
With our Saviour's generous Word Thou fillest
the Chalice of Blessing on the Christian Table of God.
O, be Thou our Life-cup on earth and become
our Eternal Life.

O wondrous Faith!
Over the deep Thou buildest Thy swinging bridge
which dares even drift ice and raging waves
from the Abode of Ghosts to the Land of the Living.
Live lowlier with us, it pleases Thee best, Thou borne-on-
      high Guest

(This may give the reader some slight impression of the Danish original.)

"Listening to the first stanza gave me real peace of mind. So did the next, because it shows that Grundtvig did not conceive the bridge of faith as something solid, but as swinging over an abyss."

I point out that, in principle, there is no difference between ending your own existence and taking the lives of all other men. That also is revealed in his dream: He kills himself but at the same time he is filled with a

[58]

gloating, malicious emotion directed at the others. In this connection I quote Kierkegaard's interpretation of Nero, how the emperor in his melancholy wished that all the heads in the entire world sat on one neck so that he could have them chopped off with one blow; I add Kierkegaard's comment that killing the entire world and killing yourself is, after all, one and the same thing.

The dream and my remarks about it make a great impression on *A*. As revealed by what he says during the rest of the session, he understands completely that the dream expresses his own strong aggression towards others, and he begins talking about the aggression which abounds in the textbook on which he is working at the moment. The book actually has taken the form of a crusade against prevailing points of view, "and heads are rolling, one after the other." He goes on to speak of his relationship with N and P. Each has his specialty which *A* never quite mastered. On the other hand, there are aspects of *A*'s field in which his two colleagues are not knowledgeable. He tells me about certain occasions on which N's or P's lack of knowledge has been laid bare, to his great delight. He also tells me of the tension which, under the surface, is present among them when together they determine examination syllabi and decide which topics are to be omitted. All in all he is making it clear to himself that a lot of aggressive tension has existed between himself and his colleagues, and that he was not willing to admit this before.

I add that this means that he wanted to represent these relationships as idyllic, completely denying the aggressive tension contained in them, that he has thus refused to perceive his relations to his close colleagues realistically as made up of both friendly and aggressive feelings. He sums up the matter by saying that certainly he realizes now that his relations to his wife as well as to his colleagues are much more complex than he has been willing to acknowledge.

He immediately goes on to recount a *dream:* He was walking the streets, and everywhere there were people standing with looks of disapproval on their faces or shaking their heads at him. It was a very unpleasant dream. Later the same night he *dreamt* that a young man threw something heavy at him from behind. He got hold of the heavy object and hurled it back at the young man, and hit him. Then he defended himself by saying that at least he had thrown from the front, while the other had hit him from behind.

He comments on these dreams without my prompting him. He says that he now realizes that he harbors so much hostility towards others, and is so critical of them, that he must face the fact that others may be aggressive and critical towards him.

V: I think that the many disapproving people in his first dream might be conceived as expressing something like: "Look, there is the man who has all those despicable, aggressive emotions." He accepts this.

Following this he talks for a long time about hospital's affairs. At first I regard this as an intermission, but he goes on to talk about the faculty's application for a professorship for him. The probable term of waiting before such an application is granted is irksome to him now. He then says that during the discussions of the student syllabus which have gone on these last few days he has admittedly had his say but was invariably frustrated, because N's opinion differs from his own, and P always sides with N, who, as *A*'s professor, in the end can, and will, overrule him. All this will change when he is a professor himself. He adds that his position is an annoying one, that he cannot help being annoyed and dissatisfied with N. "I haven't wanted to admit that kind of thing before, but must accept that that's the way it is."

He spontaneously adds that he realizes that his dream life is more active since he reduced his dose of sleeping pills to one meprobamate instead of two. He will now try to give up the last one.

December 3, 1969

A starts by telling me about the discussions concerning the new laboratory. He has become aware that budgetary application must be made for this, something N had overlooked. It is now being done.

He would like to ask me something. What should be done, in principle, about emotions which have become conscious, and which one does not want to repress? We talk in general about self-control, suppression, oblivion, and repression. All this is immediately clear and understandable to him. He especially realizes the importance of remaining conscious of emotions one had previously repressed, in the sense that one acknowledges their existence but keeps them under control and makes sure that they are no longer present as actual, disturbing emotional states. On his own initiative he adds that repression is thereby avoided, but that he previously denied the existence of conflicting emotions and would therefore suppress them on purpose.

December 5, 1969

A speaks for some time about the examination syllabus, the extent of which is to be finally decided at a meeting between him and the two professors during the next few days. It will mean a considerable enlargement of the students' curriculum. A believes that cuts should be made of sizeable sections of it in order to arrive at reasonable examination requirements for future doctors. The two professors do not share his opinion. Since the decision rests with them—especially with N, since P sides with him—this probably means that *A* cannot get his way. This is most unsatisfactory, especially as the requirements to be laid down now can hardly be altered substantially once they have been passed as a whole by the board.

Later, towards the end of the session, *A* relates a "strange, rather amusing" dream he had—it was certainly both funny and senseless, but he wants to get it told all the same, because he has taken interest in his dreams during our work with them here.

He *dreamt* that he was a bull who was to do his job, which was to mount a cow. There was a hitch, however: Both his children stood watching, holding hands and looking rather nonplussed. They were to be present as spectators, and in his dream he felt that his wife had managed this very badly. He laughs heartily while relating this dream.

In answer to my questions about his dream he says that he does not remember any actual mounting taking place, but that he felt sexually excited. He does not remember seeing the cow, but he clearly saw his children. He has no visual picture of anything bull-like about himself, but he felt like a bull, high and mighty with a large, arched neck. Laughingly he repeats that it was really a quite silly dream, which does not make any sense to him.

V: "It makes sense in that it reflects your childhood fantasies about what went on sexually between your father and mother."

A (thoughtfully): "Well, yes." The brown color of his parents' bedroom, which he previously mentioned, recurred in this dream, and the red overalls worn in it by his children were exactly the same as those he and his brother wore when they lived with some relatives on a farm where, for the first time, he saw a bull mount a cow. He must have been some six or seven years old at the time. His eldest brother was with him and had explained what was happening.

In our further discussion of this I suggest that his dream expresses his feelings, typical of a child after such an experience, at the thought of his father and mother doing the same thing as the bull and the cow. This would have aroused his curiosity, but since he disliked it, he would have repressed it. I refer to his remark—made earlier when he was describing his parents' bedroom and spoke of his mother having had her children there—that in that room his parents must have had their sexual life together, but that it was totally beyond his imaginative powers. He becomes thoughtful.

December 8, 1969

A has, he says, had the great satisfaction of succeeding in making the two professors accept his proposal of reducing the extent of the examination syllabus. A third of it will be dropped. He talks for quite a while about this.

Thereafter he tells me that on the back page of *The Christian Journal* his father was interviewed on the occasion of his turning 75. Many details of this interview demonstrate to A how much he resembles his father; most especially he latches on to the typical sharpness with which his father expresses his views, so typical of him. His emotional reaction to this aspect of his father's character is a very mixed one.

(During this session it seems obvious that at the moment A is working hard on coming to grips with the way he identifies with his father.)

December 12, 1969

Last session was cancelled by me.

"Contrary to his wont" *A* had a bad night; he was troubled in his sleep, dreaming the same thing over and over again. He was cutting out silhouettes as a present for his father's 75th birthday the following day. However, something went wrong all the time, because his cuttings turned out to contain something which might offend his father. He dreamt this over and over, woke up again and again, but at last he dreamt that he gave his son a thorough thrashing; then he fell asleep and slept well for the rest of the night. "It seems as strange as it did last time; I can't imagine why I should beat that boy." That evening he had been sitting together with his son making a booklet for him to give his grandfather for his birthday. It contained some cuttings and funny teasing texts. From time to time he would consider if there was anything in it which might give offense to his father, but no, he did not think so. When they were through, he sent his son to bed. The boy was allowed to take a bath first and was told to be quick about it, but this is something he is not good at; after 20 minutes he was still wallowing in the tub, whistling. *A* got angry and scolded, then the boy got out of the tub and went to bed.

In this connection, however, his dream of beating the boy does not make sense, *A* says.

V: "I think it makes good sense." All evening, while preparing the birthday booklet with his boy, he has been weighing how much aggression aimed at his father in the form of good-natured teasing he could get away with. His urge to get under his father's skin shows in uneasy dreams, and the final dream is the ultimate discharge of all this aggression, only the roles are reversed: The part played so often in the old days by his father

[64]

towards him is the part he plays towards his son in his dream. In this way he is able to act out actively what he formerly had to tolerate passively. This interpretation, given here in a shortened form, obviously touches a raw spot in *A*; he seems reluctant and unwilling to accept it. I do not press my interpretation. At last he says: "I have to admit, though, that at my final viva voce examination I constantly saw a picture of my father in my mind's eye, and in a frightening and unpleasant manner. By the way, he was nervous on my account for the entire duration of my university studies, and his pressure was responsible for my finishing them in seven years. Actually that was too short a time; a year more would have profited me."

December 15, 1969

A begins by saying: "Last time I was reluctant to accept your interpretation of my dream of beating my son as an expression of my own relationship to my father. I was reluctant because there is something in it which is valid for many aspects of my life." He had thought it over and realized how like his father he is: He reacts the same way, holds his father's opinions, does not really dare to have different ones, truth to say. The other evening at his father's, for instance, they discussed relations with "the church-estranged." (This is his father's customary term for people who are not actively engaged in congregational matters and who are not regular church-goers.) His father has definite views on such people, does not like them. When he has to be among such people he is unable to feel natural and at ease. *A*'s attitude is different, intellectually as well as emotionally. But in their discussion he did not so much as hint at this. "And maybe, all things considered, that was actually wiser, my father being as old as he is and hardly likely to change or understand other views than his own; but that isn't the point, because my prime reason for not speaking up was that I didn't dare contradict him. I feel that in the final analysis I do not even dare think differently. There are thus innumerable matters on which I spontaneously identify with my father. It has become quite clear to me that towards my children I often play my father's part, not least when I am angry and scold them."

Yesterday when he went to church and sat way down under the organ loft he became enmeshed in his own thoughts during the sermon. "That is to say, I didn't think of anything in particular and then suddenly I had a daydream, or whatever it was, just as vivid as a true dream. It seemed to me as if I was sitting in the chamber of a grave, one of those with a large stone slab on top of it, like a dolmen in fact. There was a small opening for light, and if I could get through that, I would be in the free, open air among all sorts of different people. I did get out that way, but very obviously against my father's wish. It was all very vivid."

Later he says that this also bears upon his relationship to his wife, because her parents belong among the "church-estranged." His father's attitude towards them is always constrained; he is artificially friendly. Really his wife is also "church-estranged," since she never went to church before they were engaged. Admittedly, going to church has become so much a part of her life that she would probably keep going even in the event of his death, but even so . . . so often she says: "That's how you feel," and by that "you" she means *A* and his father.

It suddenly comes to mind how, not long ago, one of his sisters-in-law caught sight of *A* and his brother while they were sitting side by side just before leaving the dinner table. With a laugh she pointed at them and said:

"Look, they are the spittin' image of granddaddy." They were both leaning backwards, hands folded across their bellies, as their father had always done when he finished eating.

He goes on to say that this far-reaching identification has only now become clear to him. He can also plainly see what inner conflicts it caused in his emotional attitude towards New Guinea. During his stay there he felt pressured in the same way as by his father: His point of view, on the proper way of relating to Roman Catholics and Muslims for instance, was totally at variance with that of the mission, but he felt a moral obligation to side with the mission.

"When I was a boy, my father dominated me completely, and I wanted to be like him in all respects; at puberty, however, I became very rebellious, and in my years from 16 to 20 we were hardly on speaking terms."

V: "And despite all this you have still, in many aspects, continued to identify with him. It can be easily understood how under such circumstances, a personality will be divided against itself."

Incidentally, his father was delighted at the gift of the booklet and found it amusing.

December 17, 1969

A begins by talking about an examination he held yesterday. He tried purposely to keep an emotional distance between him and the candidate, not to identify with him. In this he succeeded excellently. He felt calm and at ease, much more so than on earlier occasions; he even sensed an increase of vitality by thus being able to function with an impartial composure.

For the rest of the session he speaks at length about how he feels about his father's attitude towards life, not

[67]

least with respect to sexual matters. His father is an ardent follower of a doctor by the name of Frimodt-Moeller, who shares his religious convictions and also wrote a book entitled *Our Generative Life*. By this he meant what nowadays we would call sex life, and a main thesis of the book is that sexuality should serve procreation only. Thus, when people have had all the children they want, they should cease from sexual activity. This book is a great favorite of *A*'s father's, as well as of other members of the family who belong to the same strict branch of Danish Lutheranism. *A* does not consciously agree with views such as these, but his attitude towards them is still unclarified; he constantly finds himself carrying on an inner dialogue, seeking counter-arguments against them.

December 19, 1969

A starts by stating that he believes he has got a grip on his attitude towards sex life, or at least important aspects of it. He feels that to a large extent he has identified with his father, as he did in the dream of the bull: He saw both himself and his father in tyrannical guise, as if using force in sexual matters, with almost evil intent. This is how he has always conceived of his father's sexual relations with his mother, his father dishing out what his mother with submission had to suffer. In passing be it said that she has never been heard to hint that this aspect of life might be enjoyable. On the same conceptual lines he has himself often misused sexual actions as expressions of power, hostility even, in relation to his wife: During her premenstrual periods, when she is averse to intercourse, he has forced it upon her, more as a kind of revenge than for the sake of any real loving delight. Yet at other times it is after all very different, and his essen-

[68]

tial conception of the sexual side of conjugal life is, as he has said before, that it opens up an experience of togetherness not otherwise attainable. This, however, presupposes mutual involvement, and when she is not in the mood and holds aloof, his aggression may dominate. He discourses on the subject for some time, on how he has repressed such aggressive feelings, although they were present within him and also actively realized in his relations with his wife. I add the comment that—although what I say should not be taken as an indirect attempt to influence or pressure him—his whole attitude toward their problem of birth control is typical of his attempts to stifle his aggression, called forth by the frustration he feels when deferring to her wishes. He acknowledges the truth of this.

He speaks of his wife's clearly contradictory attitude toward birth control: She is certainly averse to pregnancy, yet she clings to a method of birth control which—as she knows—constantly exposes her to the risk of getting pregnant. Running the risk, however, is just what she wants.

While discussing whether or not his impression of his parents' sex life is realistic, he himself speculates that his own children probably have very much the same idea of his and his wife's intimate life. Coming home the other day after dinner was on the table he hugged his wife; their son immediately reacted by saying: "Do leave mama to have her dinner in peace." The boy's tone indicated, the father felt, that he was against any show of intimacy on his father's part towards his mother.

In connection with the Frimodt-Moellerian views—which as noted he does not share—he states that he still feels a great admiration for people who are able to master themselves even to the point of renouncing their sexuality completely. Thus he was deeply impressed by a passage in Gandhi's autobiography in which he recounts that at a certain stage of his life he decided to have no further sexual relations with his wife, a decision he took with her approval. He writes openly about how difficult it was. *A* found—and still finds—this to be admirable.

December 22, 1969

A tells me that on the day of our last session he caught a cold and that since then he has experienced some anxiety; it has not overpowered him, however. One night he could not sleep for anxiety. After a while the anxiety left him, but even so he could not sleep. So he took a sleeping pill; then he slept. He asks if this is reprehensible from a therapeutic point of view.

V: "No, if it is only a single tablet of meprobamate occasionally against insomnia—and not against anxiety—it is not objectionable."

Last night *A* dreamt again and again about a doctor, an assistant of his. Every time he dreamt that this man performed a certain experiment by a method they use on an apparatus available at their laboratory. Something about the doctor's experiment was constantly annoying to *A*, did not suit him.

The young doctor has actually taken measurements on this apparatus without asking *A*'s permission and this annoys him. However, *A* admits that his irritation is groundless and he cannot see, moreover, why he should be generally annoyed with the man. It is true that this summer he had a crush on the doctor's very lovely young wife, although naturally he suppressed this completely at the time because he regarded it as unseemly. Just the other day, however, he ransacked his conscience about it and acknowledged the truth. Surely that cannot be a problem, he claims, because it was not a case of falling "seriously" in love; but it has cropped up in his mind that the reason lurking behind his irritation at the doctor might be a certain jealousy. The experiment performed by the doctor in *A*'s dream involved sticking knives into a piece of body tissue. *A* was struck by the thought that this might be interpreted as the doctor having intercourse with his wife: "I believe that by now I have the formula, you know." For some reason, however, he does not really believe this himself. Be that as it may, he cannot deny that he is annoyed with the doctor, who incidentally does his best to please him and flatters him a good deal besides. Some time ago this doctor and a chemist who also works under *A* conducted some experiments which seem to disprove a theory *A* has published and for which he has received much acclaim. He took this calmly, he says. (His manner was indeed quite unruffled at the time he told me about it.) New experiments, while not quite conclusive, now tend to show that his theory is nevertheless correct.

Incidentally, and to his great astonishment, *A* has for the last few days felt no erotic desire at all for his wife, whose period is coming to its end. He does not look forward to this at all; on the contrary he feels something approaching repugnance. This is certainly a novel experience for him.

In passing he says that his wife has been in low spirits of late; why he does not know.

V: "There is no hiding, after all, that your relationship to her is not devoid of conflict, and she probably senses this, even if no words pass between you about it."

The Christmas holidays are starting now; we will meet again on Monday, January 5, 1970.

[71]

January 5, 1970

A has, he says, gained real insight into his reaction to his medical assistant. It parallels earlier relations in his life, such as the warm, almost motherly way in which he treated his Boy Scouts while he was a scoutmaster. However, at the same time he had the strange and irrational feeling that the boys ought not, really, to do anything without his permission. If, for instance, he met one of them skiing alone in the woods, he quite unreasonably felt a strange irritation that the boy had not asked leave of him to go skiing. He was conscious that his reaction was unreasonable. Such instances were many, and it is true that his reaction to this medical assistant, who had, quite unobjectionably, performed experiments on his own, was of the same kind. *A* had felt a similar unreasonable irritation with this doctor, who had made his wife pregnant: "He didn't ask my permission—after all, she was the one I had a crush on" is *A*'s comment.

I comment that in such relations he is reflecting and reenacting his father's relationship to himself. He thus relates to younger men as his father did to him, even down to the matter of the said doctor making his wife pregnant. (On returning from New Guinea *A* had a distinct feeling that his father wanted to prevent *him* from making *his* wife pregnant.)

A accepts and understands this, and he adds, "On the whole I have otherwise succeeded in transforming 'neurotic misery' into 'general misery.' Not long ago, while my wife was in her 'safe' period, I tried to make her accept a complete *coitus*." (By this *A* means *coitus* without withdrawal.) "She wouldn't."

V: "Why was that?"

A: "Well, that was because of the soiling—as I have told you, she knows her own mind. She is quite ada-

[72]

mant. On these two occasions I started to scold and make a rumpus as never before, and she was truly frightened. When I had calmed down a bit—well, I tried to be obliging, and then she too became nice and sweet.''

He tells me that while working within himself on his relationship with his medical assistant he painted a picture. The subject matter of it came to his mind spontaneously. He depicted the assistant wreaking havoc with a large phallus on a large jar, A trying to hold onto the pieces.

In a way which I cannot recall specifically, A turns to speaking of his worry lest I should try to make him act out his inclinations more recklessly than he believes himself morally able to accept.

I reply that it is rather obvious that the medical assistant in his picture also represents me. This being so, his picture would express his fear that I believe that one should whack one's phallus around dashing anything in pieces like a potter breaking his vessels with a rod of iron. I explain that this is untrue: I am against repression only, not against self-control.

January 7, 1970

A develops a theme from our last session: his urge to steer and to dominate others he now views as a result of his identification with his father and as a consequence of his father's relationship to him. (It seems clear that when speaking of this he regards his own wish to wield power as something fundamentally base.)

My comments are twofold: (1) Wielding power may, of course, result in intolerable, unrighteous tyranny, but, on the other hand, it is also conducive to much valuable and productive activity—leadership for instance. I stress that A himself has done useful work in this capacity all

[73]

his life. (2) The urge for dominance and power is without doubt a fundamental part of his own makeup, as it has been of his father's. In this respect he has not become as he is *just* because of his identification with his father.

January 9, 1970

A has given much thought to the theme we discussed last session. He has realized how important it has been to him to control others, and that this trait has been productive of good as well as of other things. For instance, it is now clear to him that the part of his present work which means most to him is lecturing. When he is successful, as he often is, he finds great satisfaction in spellbinding his audience, so that each and every head turns to following his motions as he crosses from one end of the blackboard to the other. He works intensely on his lectures to achieve this end. It was the same in missionary circles, when he sensed that he could enthrall an audience. He has also felt deeply frustrated when, as once in France, he was unable to catch the full attention of his audience because they understood him with difficulty, or not at all. Likewise, the greatest disappointment of his life may have been the discovery that in New Guinea white men were barred from preaching to the natives. This was the exclusive right of the native ministers—who are, by the way, singularly eloquent. To the native mind listening to another person means submitting oneself to him, and for this reason preaching is not entrusted to white men. When, as often happens, a white person helps a native minister with the content of his sermon, it is all very hush-hush.

A: "However, dominating an assembly in such a masterful way has something perilous to it—I sensed that

[74]

acutely in a *dream* I had last night: I was in a church delivering a sermon, standing in the pulpit—I have actually done so several times—and I was quite carried away by my own eloquence. But then I saw the shadow of a horned devil projected on the opposite wall, and my words reverberated from this shadow on the wall back to the congregation so that it seemed it was the devil speaking. His horns were the reflection of a crown I was wearing: I had been crowned by the congregation. What I had just been expounding dealt with the crown of thorns worn by Our Lord.'' From what he adds it is apparent that he completely realizes the implications of his dream, even to the detail that the figure of the devil touches on his childhood picture of his father as a devil from hell shoveling coal into the furnace. He says that the voice reverberating from the shadow on the wall was his father's.

As an example of the significance he attaches to dominating an audience while addressing it he emphasizes that becoming a professor—as almost certainly he will by April 1971—has lost most of its attraction for him. This is because the premises which will be his will not contain an auditorium. Thus for his lectures he will have to borrow one, live on loan so to speak.

January 12, 1970

A recounts a *dream:* In it he was a boy and he was walking hand in hand with either his father or me—which it was could not be determined—across the square where his father garaged his car every day. He caught sight of a large yellow bird with a huge bill which had been laced up so that it could not emit a sound. At the same time it was being vexed and teased by a small bird flitting around it. Later, however, it was as if the

[75]

large bird was taken in by someone, had the cord removed from its bill, and was given something to eat. He surmises that the large bird is himself and that the small one may be his medical assistant.

I advance no interpretation of the dream. It is rather obvious that it expresses an emotional transference from his father to me, and that this entails a blocking of verbal expressions of aggression towards me. But being unable to quote any actual instance thereof on which to base an interpretation, I refrain from comment.

Incidentally, he talks at length about having visited his father during the past weekend and having a long talk with him. He states that their relationship has improved markedly, and that he is now able to talk to his father without feeling tense. He feels a good sense of contact with him.

He goes on to speak about his attitude towards the professorship he will now probably get. He pictures it in rather drab colors, he says; this is partly because the lack of an auditorium vexes him, but also because research, although he does a considerable amount of it, is not his primary interest. Teaching is what he really likes.

January 14, 1970

A dreamt that he was visiting London together with an uncle for a real fling. They had already played some huge practical joke; but what it was, specifically, he cannot remember. On top of this they had decided to rent Christine Keeler for a night. (She was the hooker who shook the British cabinet when it was exposed that she had been joint mistress of the Secretary of State for War, Mr. Profumo, and a Russian military attaché.) However, they let her down. Her manager arrived and he was upset, because she would thus lose a whole night's profit—£600. So in the end *A* took her along in his car. She began to make up to him with almost repulsive, snake-like movements, to which he did not respond. She complained of this and said what she wanted was a really hungry, starved man—sexually speaking. He then drove her to some place in Soho, where a whole bunch of very vulgar, sozzled men were loafing. He handed her over to them despite her screaming protests. They hurled themselves upon her with avid glee, eyes popping out of their heads and hands greedily pawing her. One of them cried out that, after all, there was no sense in sharing her, but the others shouted him down: everyone could take his share. *A* was having fun. At this moment his father shook him by the shoulder with laughing appreciation—something he would never do in reality.

The dream seems clear to *A* himself. It expresses his newly won, much more complex vision of his wife. "Actually I feel a loathing for her. This is partly—but not only—because of our sexual difficulties. More general aspects of her personality are involved too." At the same time he feels deep affection for her, and now he does not regard these attitudes as conflicting. Previously he willed himself to view their marriage as inanely blissful. He does not do so any longer.

V: "You are wont to describe your wife as a very determined person whom one cannot budge from her intent." Sexually this shows in the determined way in which she sets limits that he may not transgress. Part of his satisfaction in his dream presumably stems from his delivering her up with abandon to the completely uninhibited.

A: "Yes, precisely to that element in myself."

A had another *dream*, which he does not understand: he was performing for a large crowd which he held in awe by an experiment. His son participated in the role of a crier of sorts. The experiment involved his standing on some peat piled high which it was difficult to balance on. It was part of the experiment that the pile suddenly disappeared from under him. When that happened, he slid down a high tree trunk, slightly bruising his hands. Then he was standing on a beach by the ocean down in Kenya. Suddenly a lot of other men were sliding down palm trees, and then I (V), too, was present, spick-and-span in the uniform of a British officer, telling them that this was an extremely important moment, when apes ceased to be apes and became humans and came down from the trees. Then they all, A included, had to form a line, because a company had to be sent off on account of trouble in Rhodesia. This dream makes no sense to A.

I say that nevertheless some main themes of importance to him can be discerned in it: on the one hand his wish for satisfaction through domination of others; on the other its antithesis, taking his place alongside many others under a master. This is closely connected with his relationship with both his father and myself as expressed in his dreams of late. They both show contradictory attitudes. After all, even the first, satisfying dream contains the point that by performing a reckless act of a sexual nature, directed, so to speak, by me, he will make me happy. In the dream he narrated last session, the one in which he went hand in hand with a person who was at the same time his father and me, he was also a bird with its bill tied up. Now, in his latest dream, his control of many persons abruptly changes into my control of him as only one of many. He should take notice of this side of his attitude to me, and of the part he ascribes to me as his seducer; its footprint keeps showing up.

A accepts this reflectively. He then says that he believes the others sliding down the trees were professors, and that the falling into line is expressive of his feelings towards being a professor. It is true that, on reflection, he increasingly discerns the good side to it; nevertheless, its main connotation for him is of being penned up, confined to a somatic approach, and shut off from many more general human goals to which he would like to make a contribution.

V: "Well, to you a professorial appointment clearly signifies giving up your ancient dream of becoming a hero."

A: "Exactly so, and now the life I led and the possibilities I had in New Guinea glow with radiant light compared to a humdrum professorship."

V: "Be that as it may, when you first came to me, you described the part you played in New Guinea in anything but radiant terms. In fact, what you depicted was an all encompassing disappointment because you were unable to become the hero you expected to be."

A (laughingly): "That is true enough." Incidentally, when he was a small boy, his teacher once asked the pupils what they would like to be when they grew up. It was at the time of life when they all wanted to become firemen, train guards, or something like that. To the hilarity of everybody he answered that he wanted to be a conductor of an orchestra.

V: "Well, that must have been your idea of a hero at the time."

A: "Yes. I even asked my mother how I could become one, and she answered me seriously and factually. In former times being a professor was a far greater thing than it is today. At that time a professor had the power to shape the content of his entire discipline; but now come the boards with their student members and all the ensuing bother."

When we had talked for a time about the clash between his old hero-fantasies and the day-to-day activities

[79]

of a professor, *A* finished by saying: "On the other hand, one might regard it as the starting point of the true task of one's manhood."

January 16 and 19, 1970

A talks of his feelings about becoming a professor. It has become clear to him that his early conception of a professor was a person living in some mansion in a very posh street in central Copenhagen and being driven in a coach and four. While on vacation from New Guinea he took an exclusive course with a professor and observed how unpretentiously his instructor lived. The luster of being a professor waned considerably. Even so, and despite the knowledge that what power and influence he may possibly come to wield must be far inferior to that of a professor of a bygone age, it has in recent days become increasingly clear to him that the post which will become the main task of his life holds important and worthwhile possibilities.

January 26, 1970

Yesterday *A* held his last viva voce examination of this term. Soon he is to make plans for his new department. He is now keen to do this and feels up to being a professor. He claims that our discussions have helped him to adapt himself to these questions far more quickly than he could otherwise have done.

January 28, 1970

A dreamt as follows: His children had fitted up some small boxes lined with hay (like pigsties on a farm) in which they were playfully wallowing just like pigs.

[80]

However, they had also, pig-fashion, arranged a place in a corner of the box to pee in. This angered him, and he sternly ordered them not to do it. All the same he saw that his son peed in the corner again. In his dream he then went berserk and beat up the boy in the same un-controlled, brutal way he had done in an earlier dream. His unprovoked comment is that he knows well what triggered it. The evening before he had told his son to hurry up in the bathroom, he wanted a bath himself. However, the boy did not hurry; on the contrary he dallied, probably on purpose, to tease. Good a boy as he is, at the moment he is in a determined, defiant phase, and *A* does his best not to coerce him overtly. The boy is patently jealous of *A*'s relations with his wife; he wants his mother for himself and interrupts his parents in a conspicuous way when they are talking together. When *A* comes home after dinner is served and kisses his wife, his son cuts in saying: "Daddy, leave mama to her din-ner." A few days ago the boy also heard him ask his wife if they could not go to bed early. When she answered: "Sure, but you know we are going to sleep straight away," *A* retorted: "In that case I shall take a bath; I can have that, at any rate."

He then talks about his research. At the moment he has time for it and he enjoys doing it. He touches on a project which he and two other doctors are working on together. The difficulty is that while he has completed his part, an extensive analysis of data including statistics and so on, the other two have not been able to get their part written for publication. As his tale unfolds it be-comes clear to me that quite possibly he is being too considerate. One of the two colleagues has been sitting on the raw material for two years, and *A* could easily insist on having it back and finish the article on his own. As to the other, *A* needs this doctor's cooperation for some clinical details, but in this case he could undoubtedly apply more pressure than he has seen fit to do. I tell him this in the form of a comment to the effect that it might be opportune if, in his reaction to these two, he would use but a slight amount of that direct, person-to-person aggression which he shows towards his son in his dream. On the basis of this I stress, as I have done before, that obviously he is not at all a mild person through and through. He feels uncomfortable about aggressive self-assertion towards individuals; when it comes to institutions he can be very different, quite impetuous, as well he knows.

At one point during the session he remarks that lately it has dawned on him that he has experienced anxiety states at various periods of his life, such as when, at the age of 26 or 27, he went to America. He traveled by train to Hamburg. While crossing Zealand he sustained a violent attack of panic of the same kind as the one last summer.

He has since, on different occasions, felt an anxiety which could not readily be explained by the existing situation. He had attacks of panic as a child too, not least at night when his mother would have to calm him down.

January 30, 1970

A immediately tells me that by losing his head he has suddenly clashed violently with Professor P.

The day before yesterday a meeting was held between departments C and D. Some joint conferences held every other week were on the agenda. A belongs to the department of which N is the chief. P is the chief of department C. N was absent from the meeting. The topic of these meetings has hitherto been narrowly specialized out of consideration for the interests of department C. However, this topic holds no interest for the staff of department D; they know little about it and cannot keep up. Consequently, D's staff has been unable to profit from the conferences. A set forth this grievance at the meeting, gaining the support of all those who expressed their opinion, including some of P's own staff. His motion to change entirely the form and content of these conferences was consequently passed against the wish of Professor P.

When, yesterday, for other reasons, he popped into Professor P's office, having dismissed the matter completely from his thoughts, he found P in quite a state. P blew his top, in sharp terms venting disapproval at what had happened as well as at the manner in which A had seen fit to plead his cause. Actually P took his argument far afield and blamed A for things he has had no influence on. Moreover, he claimed that he and his staff generally had the impression that A was very "destructive"—a term he used over and over.

A was quite taken aback, albeit he freely admits to having set forth his case somewhat awry. Without giving the matter a thought he had been teasing—and he is good at that. It had made everyone laugh at P and, on reflection, A admits that it was quite the wrong thing to do to P, who cannot reply in kind and feels helpless in the face of an attack of this sort. With N one can very well have a showdown of this kind—he can give as good as he takes.

As to the concrete situation at the meeting the day before, A made penance, saying that he was sorry for the offense he had given to P. However, he repudiated P's other allegations, denying that he could be guilty of things he had not had anything to do with, and P admitted that these accusations were unwarranted. Something

[83]

remained, however: *A* had heard even from his own subordinates that the staff of department C had not felt welcome when the department was established, and *A* has the feeling that to a large extent they blamed him for it. Thus the accusations of "destructiveness" may contain a grain of truth, however much they come as surprise to him.

As we discuss this I once more stress that when it comes to aggression he maintains a double standard. Towards individuals he is willfully unaggressive—and pictures himself as such—even to the extent of feeling uncomfortable in his role of examiner because it necessitates doing harm, however justified, to individual persons who do not pass. When he deals with institutions or "business," however, he allows his strong, underlying aggressive tendencies full play. It is equally obvious that his aggression may take an indirect, jocular form, in a way which his victim interprets as an unprovoked and hostile act—to *A*'s own great surprise. What is to be dwelt upon is his surprise when others are piqued by his remarks, because he is probably aggressive in a similar way in many other connections without its being clear to himself. This is something to which he should direct his attention. The reason for doing so is not, I add, that offending others can be said to be undesirable or reprehensible in a general sense; but it is certainly a good thing to know when one is doing it.

February 2, 1970

A has given much thought to his difficulties: He is sure they are not the simple result of the conditions under which he has to live; he contributes actively to them himself, as may be seen in this confrontation with P. He recalls my reiterated statement that he is a naturally passionate and aggressive person and he would be the last to deny it. But, after all, that should not mean that this aggressive nature of his must perforce lead him into such predicaments as it has often done in the past. It cannot be that his destiny is dictated by his character to this extent. It ought to be possible to manage these tendencies in other ways. He feels himself split in two and he senses that fear is the reason for his frequent losses of temper—a fear which has its roots in an unwillingness to accept himself as he truly is.

Yesterday, a Sunday, he went to church and once more pondered these questions. In church, more particularly when receiving the Eucharist, he experiences a calm he does not know in daily life. That is not to say that his problems vanish—how could they?—but somehow they dissolve. He knows that it sounds vague, because words are inadequate, but he does grow calm. "That is because there I am allowed to be a sinner, I should say a criminal even, and yet receive grace and forgiveness."

He develops this theme at some length, claiming that it ought to be possible in the ordinary run of life to feel the same calm as he does during Holy Communion, acknowledging that one is judged guilty but in a state of grace and therefore without fear. "But difficult it is. Just a short while after I returned from church I flared up inside and came out with a sour remark aimed at my wife, because lunch was ready only at a quarter past twelve. You know I have this thing about meals being served on the dot. Of course I realize that it doesn't make sense. My wife is always at least ten minutes late, and I might as well accept her as she is—always a little late. We have only rarely been able to leave for a train on time; we always have to catch it at a run at the last second. But that's how she is, and why not just put up with it?"

[85]

Having acknowledged that this seemed important to him, he was disturbed in his sleep nevertheless. Among other things he *dreamt* that he had been condemned to decapitation; however, they kept deferring the actual execution. He had even written an appeal in which he offered to serve at his father's table for the rest of his life if only he could be reprieved. A jailer told him that there was not much of a chance of such a petition doing him any good—better have his head chopped off as quickly as possible. He then saw people laying a table at which his father and brothers would be sitting for a grand dinner in celebration of his beheading. He woke up with a ghastly feeling.

The night before he had *dreamt* that by changing a neon tube at his department he had offended both the ministry and the electricians. The electricians then grabbed him, set him on a table, and tied him up with a lot of cables, some of which they made into a crown of thorns they put on his head. You could just press the button, they said—then he would die. However, they left without doing so. Commenting on this dream, he tells me that just now they have electricians working at the hospital, and that he got them to do a little wiring for him which he needed but which, strictly speaking, was not part of their proper assignment.

I make no comments on these dreams, nor on what he says as he goes on. He remarks that such problems may certainly trouble him, but that this bears no relation to his attacks of panic. The unpleasantness he now feels is something he can work on. The attacks appeared as isolated, inexplicable, and unmanageable events.

He goes on to talk of his 14-year-old daughter, who has a girl friend of the same age. This girl seems to have a great interest in sex and claims that she takes her boy friend to bed. "But maybe she is just shooting her mouth off." He has heard his wife talk to their daughter about it and he finds that she does it well, not acting the scaremonger but guiding her realistically and sensibly.

February 4 and 6, 1970

During these two sessions A talked about professional matters. Furthermore, he spoke about his attitude towards the Christian religion in general, pondering whether or not it is fundamentally different from other religions. He is not inclined to believe so himself; however, such a point of view is undeniably at variance with that held in missionary circles.

February 9, 1970

A confines himself to various reflections of a general nature. (Some subject seems to be about to break through, but he balks at it. It is my guess that it is problems involving dominance and submission among males. I have lately considered whether A has reached a point where we might cut down on the frequency of his sessions and maybe shortly terminate treatment; symptomatically he is well and has reached a considerable insight, along with radically changing his attitude toward himself and his situation. However, I have constantly kept in mind that problems of male dominance and submission have not been dealt with in any real sense.)

February 13, 1970

A tells me of his problem with O, a younger doctor subordinate to him, who has given him disciplinary problems before. Yesterday a colloquium was held according to a new procedure which A forced upon the other department. Therefore, it was vital that it be a success. At their request *A* had left to O and another of his assistants the presentation of the subject to be discussed, and had told them to speak for 20 minutes each; just before the beginning of the meeting he had repeatedly impressed on O that it was imperative that he confine himself to the 20 minutes allotted to him. Nevertheless, he spoke for an hour and 20 minutes, appeared rather confused, lost the gist of his argument time and again, and miswrote on the blackboard. The whole thing fell apart, and the audience, which was suffering as time dragged on, was repeatedly eying *A:* Putting an end to it, if that had to be done, was, after all, his responsibility. His other assistant kept scrupulously within his 20 minutes. *A* made no comment to O on his performance right away. Later O asked him what he thought about it. *A* started by saying something nice about the good things he had said, and O was inordinately pleased with this. *A* then added: ''Maybe it lasted a bit too long,'' a remark which O pooh-poohed. *A* did not come straight to the point, for instance by saying how far he had exceeded his time limit, something O did not even seem to be sensible of. Nor did *A* reproach him for speaking unprepared as he did. *A* felt extremely uncomfortable about it all; he actually felt anxiety afterwards.

I comment that the situation is typical: In a direct face-to-face encounter of a personal nature he hesitates to show aggression even to the point of frustrating himself and omitting measures which, as the person ultimately responsible, it is his duty to take, out of consideration for the rest of the audience. I add that this is not said in order to indicate any precise method of action to be followed in such cases; I only want to draw up the outlines of a problem, because it is pertinent to him.

A sees this clearly; when he recoils from speaking up

and giving O the dressing-down he so richly deserves, it is because he knows that this would hurt O deeply.

V: "You are obviously identifying with O, empathizing with him through the feelings you would have yourself, if you were made the target of such criticism."

A becomes very thoughtful at this and talks it over for some time. He perceives the existence of some basic problem. I put in a remark to the effect that the situation with O contains matter vital to his problems. He won't deny this, he says; nevertheless, he is of the opinion that if some particular attitude in life is of paramount importance to you, for instance to be considerate towards others, then it will affect your feelings and doings in all manner of different situations.

V: "This attempt of yours to generalize what is concrete, thereby reducing it in significance, is surely a sign of resistance, a result of the distaste—vague and unexpressed as it may be—you feel at the thought of having to deal in greater detail with the emotions and ideas lurking behind your reaction to O." I remind him that he has tried similar subterfuges before, for instance when he would belittle the sexual problems he has with his wife.

A (with a smile): "How right you are!" After thinking some more about it he says: "Well, this thing with O—I believe I can fathom it to some extent. There has to be something erotic involved. That is clear to me, visibly even, from the picture I painted of him recently: there was this penis-like figuration crossing the painting." I ask him to bring along the picture next session. He promises to do so.

While discussing his relationship with O, *A* said he would think that these problems are somewhat similar to what I once touched upon in connection with ranking order among male baboons and the way they demonstrate their submission to one another. The weaker male of lesser rank signifies his submission to the stronger by assuming the stance of a female in heat, the floor of the pelvis exposed, ready for covering: *presenting* as the zoologist's technical term has it. (It is correct that I once briefly mentioned this, in order, among other things, to leave *A* an opening for a not too affect-ridden approach to problems of dominance and submission. This was some time ago.)

February 16, 1970

A had a *dream* about O which has given him an understanding of a good many things which troubled him before, but no longer do so.

He was riding a bus, sitting beside the driver. Suddenly O ran out in front of the bus and lay down with obvious suicidal intent. Shocked, *A* tried to make the driver stop, but in vain. He just ran O over, and a horrible crunching sound was heard as he did it. The driver then jumped down from the bus and now it was his turn to lie down in front of it and be run over. Afterwards *A* saw O and the driver jumping about in screaming pain with horridly maimed heads. It was a frightful dream.

A claims that in a flash this dream made him understand his relationship with O, who irritates him by being ingratiating in a servile manner. At times this has filled him with downright loathing. He now realizes that his dream reveals his own inclination towards subduing and maltreating O, also that this inclination is partly of a sexual nature. The mere thought of anything sexual in relation to other men has always seemed intolerable to him, but now he understands that such sexual feelings are part of his nature. This realization has eased the tension he felt about these matters.

[90]

Following this up, I emphasize that with this in mind his reluctance to take O to task when necessary becomes understandable. Emotionally he is unable to distinguish between such level-headed reproof on the one hand, and on the other submitting O to a gross, unrestrained show of brute force of a sexual sort, threatening him with humiliation, even mutilation. This undercurrent of far-reaching fantasies and impulses frightens him—thus making him abstain from even a limited display of aggression, though called for by the realities confronting him—witness his trouble with O.

A: "Earlier, in cases where I had achieved insight into something, I dreamt that I had created something really beautiful. I did so in this case too. I *dreamt* that I had done a large, gilded relief for a youth center. My sculpture was to be hung in the hall. It represented a woman helping a man onto a bedpan"—this with a grin.

After waking up from this dream he lay pondering the picture he had painted of O's penis. He has brought the painting along today. It came home to him that now it was fully comprehensible to him in all its details: From left to right stretches the large, red, pointed penis, which is broken midways by a large, white aggressive cone, smiting it from above. From the sundered penis blood spurts down on both sides, running through and fertilizing verdant meadows. Thus destruction becomes creative of new life. The phallus isn't only O's, it is *A*'s own as well. In order to explain all this *A* is searching for the right words, and his explanation strikes me as far from airy speculation. In the top left corner there is a splash of violet indicating the wrath of God, which is atoned for by the broken penis. To the right, below the "crack" in the red phallus a dark rectangular spot is seen; it is the vulva, another creator of life. Down to the left are four yellow squares, which are windows in a

[91]

house where he and his wife are living happily. The large eye at the top left is his own, while the puny one at the right is O's. The yellow cone at the center is a tent of the kind the telephone company puts across their trenches; it is also the department where he works. On completing this explanation *A* looks a little lost, commenting that after all it's not so easy to explain that sort of thing sensibly. I answer that I perfectly well understand his interpretation of the picture as a cosmic drama. "Yes, that's exactly what it is," he eagerly exclaims.

Without any prompting from me he stresses that neither the painting nor the episode with O, in all its aspects, should be seen as something isolated. On the contrary, his relationship with O is a particular case which mirrors his relationships with males in general.

As he continues talking about homosexual inclinations and what they mean to him, about how the mere thought of anything of the kind has always stood in his imagination as something totally unacceptable, I interpose that the homosexual element in interrelations between males is not limited to sexual gratification and wielding power. I then explain to him that the homosexual inclinations felt by boys and younger men towards older boys and men are basic facts of human nature, and that they play an important educational part in male development, the younger man assuming the role of an apprentice to the older, so to speak. In this connection I explain to him the symbolic meaning of the phallus.

February 18, 1970

A arrives in high spirits and begins by saying that he just has to share his joy with me. A. L. Hansen has informed him that their experiments now truly appear to be a success. The treatment has just that therapeutic effect on

[92]

children which was predicted by *A*. Very naturally *A* gives me a rather detailed description of what it is all about. If A. L. Hansen's confidence in the validity of the results proves justified, it will be a momentous achievement of great practical importance, which will enable doctors to prevent the development of auto-immune defects in infants. In addition the results are of considerable theoretical interest.

He tells me with a laugh that to tell the truth he was rather annoyed with his wife because of her skeptical depreciation when he told her of it on returning home. But then she is probably a bit downcast from no longer sharing in his work as she did before.

Towards the end of the session he relates that he told his wife something about what I taught him last session about Greek homosexuality—and she, too, found it interesting. Reminiscing about his Boy Scout days he claims there was all too much denunciation of homosexuality. The terror of homosexuality was so great that among scoutmasters you did not dare admit that you might find the boys beautiful and attractive to look at. He says that in such discussions he had asserted time and again that honestly in his opinion such a youngster might be both beautiful and a moving sight, and that he couldn't for the life of him see anything wrong in that. At times the reaction to his remarks was one of consternation and virtuous indignation. In one case a fellow scoutmaster had given it to him straight that what he said was tantamount to admitting he was a homosexual. Naturally he hotly denied this. He speaks as if he has reached the conviction that emotions of this kind are part and parcel of the human condition, realizing of course that, set as we are in the mold of our particular culture, they require a considerable degree of suppression.

[93]

February 20, 1970

A starts by saying that he might as well own that he had a bad night; not nearly as bad as earlier, he hastens to add, but with feelings of anxiety nevertheless, so that he was sleepless after waking up around one o'clock. "Truth to tell you are the bee in my bonnet." He is searching for words and, shifting his seat, confesses: "Words come hard." I voice a few faint, encouraging sounds and inanities, and then he blurts out that he has been ruminating on what, "out of the kindness of your heart you once called my small neurosis: maybe it is not so small at that." He had no idea that the treatment would be so lengthy, could not imagine that I would be so patient. Since he is still susceptible to anxiety he has a nagging fear that it may have some irreparable foundation. After a little further probing of his thoughts he claims he is preoccupied with my reaction to the painting he showed me last time, or maybe he should say lack of reaction.

"True, that may be due to the matter-of fact way you handle such things; but others, such as my parents-in-law, who saw it while it was drying on the easel, expressed their opinions about it in a far more straight-forward manner. In your case I had the feeling that you understood it as a coherent whole—much better than your comments would indicate. And generally speaking, my analysis has brought to light so much that cannot at all be reconciled with my earlier thoughts and convictions."

A talks on a little while, and gradually it becomes quite apparent—as it already was at the mention of the painting—that what irks him is the homosexual material which has emerged of late. In this connection he now also feels a distinct fear of dependency in his relation-

ship to me. In passing he remarks that as a result of the
most recent sessions here his relationship with O is now
tuned down. All in all he has profited immensely from
the treatment: his relationship with his father has
changed radically and is free of tension; also with his
wife he has achieved a far healthier relationship.

I latch onto his last remarks, specifically about his
father and O, pointing out that problems similar to those
he has had in these relationships are now beginning to
show in his attitude towards me as a sense of insecurity.
He admits this and adds that last night, when he was
giving me and his treatment so much restless thought,
he had found encouragement after all in the thought that
he was capable of maintaining so close and important a
relationship to a person whose opinions and attitude to
life are as blatantly different from his own as mine are.

V: "That is true, but it also makes for insecurity. Already long ago it came up when you feared being influenced by me in your religious life, against your true
convictions."

A: "Yes, and I was also scared of being pressured into
treating my wife differently from the way I felt to be
right."

V: "Well, now the question of who is to have the
upper hand has obviously assumed paramount importance; it is something you seem to find alarming, sens-
ing, it would appear, that I hold the ascendency, while
you are submissive."

A: "That is true enough, but, after all, that follows
from the intrinsic nature of a treatment of this kind. As
you once told me yourself, it was dire necessity which
made me enter into a relationship of this kind and lay
myself bare in a way I would never have done to any
other human being."

V: "Yes. Apparently this touches on what for the sake

[95]

of convenience could be called your homosexual problem in relation to me—just to pick up the thread from your remarks last session."

A (fidgeting): "I suppose the whole set-up resembles the one I witnessed once on Hyde Park Corner where a man, speaking from a soap box, was constantly interrupted by someone in the audience. Finally he told the heckler off, shouting: 'You just have to assume the female position and let yourself be penetrated.' "

V: "That's a very apt illustration of the way problems of power among men find expression in sexual imagery. By the way, it has a parallel in the relationship between a speaker and his audience as you know it from New Guinea." (He previously mentioned that there the audience is conceived of as submitting to the speaker's authority.) I point out to him how the most recent sessions have revealed the two extremes of rank and power side by side: First his treatment of P and the dream of O and the bus expressed his violent, maiming subjugation of other men, now, conversely, he fears being himself subjected to the like treatment by me.

During our talk I remarked that vital problems such as these, relevant to the analysis of each and every male, must find expression in relation to the therapist, too.

A: "However true that may be, it is far easier to deal with them in relation to others."

February 23, 1970

I had to cancel last session.

The night after last session *A* had a *dream* he found most enlightening: He was in bed with his wife and about to have intercourse with her. He was endowed with a huge, unearthly size phallus. Now he was truly going to demonstrate his inordinate powers. He was in-

[96]

terrupted, however, by the arrival of four men like hospital orderlies, who were to carry off the bed. He could
not quite make out who they were or where they came
from. There was one especially at the head of the bed
whom he could not see—"That would have to be you."
He remonstrated loudly at this interruption. They were
going to lift up his bed and carry him off with it. He
fought the three he could see, but to no avail. Somehow
his wife had disappeared. Nor did she, properly speaking, have anything to do with what was happening. Now
he perceived that, in spite of his resistance, the men
lifted the bed and carried it down a long corridor. He
saw himself lying in it, not in his own likeness, but in the
form of an elongated, coffin-like gypsum object, which
was severed neatly and precisely into eight parts by lon-
gitudinal and transverse sections.

This dream seems to *A* immediately comprehensible
as a follow-up on last session's discussion of his fear of
me. He is convinced that it expresses the apprehension
he has, after all, been feeling all along that the treatment
here might cause a blurring of his individuality and end
up by changing him into something not himself at all,
just a mean of my idea of what a human being should be
like.

V: "So you were afraid that after treatment you would
emerge as an article mass-produced according to a pattern of psychoanalytic concepts."

A (laughing): "Precisely: something akin to that object in the bed, regular and impersonal in form and meti-
culously mapped out." It goes without saying, he adds,
that this fear is utterly groundless—that has become
quite clear to him—and the imagery of this dream strikes
him as illustrative, in a liberating way, of his erroneous
attitude.

Later on in the session *A* talks about reading Schroedinger's book, *Mind and Matter*. I lent it to him some time ago, when he mentioned the notion held by some scientists that consciousness may be a phenomenon not restricted to humans but may even conceivably extend to so-called dead matter. It takes him such a long time to read about subjects of this sort, he says. They pose so many essential questions which require close thinking. He adds that earlier in his life he had always avoided reading about such matters, been afraid of them because they might shake him in his strict missionary outlook on life.

V: "Yes, and that was because of a fear that the mass-produced missionary view you held of yourself and the world at large might crack up."

A (with a laugh): "Precisely."

February 25, 1970

A claims that now he feels cured. He has never been able to say so truthfully before, but lately, after the un-earthing of the tension with O and his own emotions in relation to me, he firmly believes that he may do so. He feels well-balanced emotionally; his condition is one of well-being, and his everyday affairs are shaping up better, at the hospital too.

Naturally that is not to say that his life has become a bed of roses. Some problems remain, "not least my relationship with my wife, but that comes under the heading of general, not neurotic, misery." The gist of it is that he wishes he had the gift to keep her better satisfied, not just sexually but in a general way. Last evening when they were discussing plans for their summer holidays, he sensed that she could not really muster any enthusiasm for his proposals, no matter what they were. After a while he said that it was a shame that nothing seemed to

make her truly happy. No doubt she took this as a reproach. He woke up once during the night and recalled
it with annoyance. Incidentally, she is in her erotically
unresponsive phase just now: "So for the moment it is
all she can do to show me a little loving affection in the
morning when I am about to leave, and she doesn't run
the risk of any consequences."

He has dreamt about a madman—it was that doctor
who caused him such trouble in New Guinea by his psy-
chopathic behavior—who pursued him and some others
gun in hand. This makes him reflect that he never liked
it much when the children were playing with guns or
other martial toys. However, he has always kept his dislike under control and let them do as they pleased. I
remark that this attitude toward violence even in play is
typical of people with symptoms of anxiety.

March 2, 1970

At the start of the session *A* says that the late time of his
appointment is somewhat of an embarrassment to him.
As I know, he has all the time been unwilling to tell N
that he is being treated by me, and now N has been
around several times to have a talk with him before he
arrived. And Wednesdays and Fridays he unavoidably is
an hour late. (I cannot take him earlier.) He adds, however, that he has no intention of making any demands or
trying to force me into making a change.

He again talks about his wife. There are sides of her
personality which bother him. In the company of aca-
demics, for instance, she experiences a certain sense of
insecurity, and now that she no longer shares in his
work, having quit the hospital's staff, she feels left out of
things. In general she harbors some discontent at being

"only" a full-time housewife. From time to time it makes her assert herself on behalf of wives. It annoys him. Yesterday evening a cousin of *A*'s paid them a visit. This man is now a professor at the Royal Academy of Arts and he and *A* played a lot together in their boyhood. *A* hadn't seen him since. Recently they ran into each other by chance, and *A* invited him. He had been looking forward to exchanging boyhood recollections with him—talking about how they played together in their grandmother's garden and so on. This came to nothing, however, because his cousin proved to have provided himself with a wife so babbling that he was unable to put in a single word all evening. He didn't get around to talking with his cousin about the things he wanted to at all. During their visit he made no show of his feelings, of course, but when they left, he grumbled at his cousin's bothersome wife. *A*'s wife then sided with the woman in quite aggressive terms—which didn't lessen his annoyance. He woke up in the night with a vehement feeling of irritation at his wife. This irritation was accompanied by a stirring of emotion, which—as he clearly perceived—would in earlier days have thrown him headlong into a state of panic. Now, however, he is conscious of being in control of things.

(The way *A* talks about his difficulties in connection with coming as often as he does seems to me to imply that he has reached the point where he would wish for a reduction of the number of sessions a week. That he does so wish seems supported by his claim to have achieved insight into his fundamental conflicts with his wife and, indeed, to have mastered them, as well as by his statements these past sessions that now he has his condition and his life in general under control. I had foreseen that something of the kind would crop up: For one thing, to the best of my knowledge, he is right when he says that his condition has greatly improved, that he is free of symptoms, and that he has achieved considerable, even revolutionary, insight into his previous inner conflicts. Furthermore I had a hunch that he might balk at further analysis of his conflicts around dominance and submission in relation to me. These are matters into which he has acquired considerable insight; an intensified overhaul of them might be worthwhile, that is evident. At the same time it is a moot point whether it is reasonable to persist along these lines, considering his very real improvement, not only with regard to his symptoms but also in insight into his character problems. I feel interest, and some curiosity too, in seeing how he will manage, if at this juncture I should indulge his desire to cut down on the frequency of sessions. I decide to do so.)

As the result of the above considerations I put it to *A* directly whether he would wish to come less frequently. He promptly answers that a cut to once a week is the very thing he has been toying with in his thoughts. However, he has not wanted to propose it directly, since he knows full well that on earlier, similar occasions he misjudged his situation. I reply that I now consider a reduction to once a week justifiable. That should be Monday, then, when I am able to see him early, so he won't have to be late to work. This pleases him very much, in what I feel is a balanced and reasonable way.

March 9, 1970

A appears to be in a happy mood. He makes no mention of any recurrence of his symptoms during the week. (I had not expected any and don't question him about it, as I do not want him to get the impression that I had anticipated any trouble.) He tells me about a brainstorm he had: He wants the scope of his future professorship narrowed to a certain specialty. He speaks about it in a way which seems relevant. Shortly after he saw me last time he *dreamt* that he was with me in a sickroom at a hospital. He was about to be discharged and was told to pack up his things and move them out. "I was to take the bed with me—a detail I don't catch the meaning of."

V: "Arise, and take up thy bed, and go thy way into thine house."

A: "Oh, of course. It has to be that." In his dream he was then standing outside the hospital with his things, luggage and all, watching me reenter the hospital with a group of patients. At that a wistful sadness crept over him at no longer belonging among those who went in with me.

He interprets his dream as a plain, undisguised expression of a feeling of sadness at being about to end his treatment with me.

Talking of a comedy he saw, staged by his son and some of pals of his, he holds forth about the attraction a life among boys holds for him and recalls his time as a Boy Scout master with some nostalgia. He then says this was the cause of his first disagreement with his wife, as she quite definitely disliked the fellowship he shared with the other masters and was absolutely averse to joining up herself as she could so easily have done. So in the end, and in short while at that, he had to give it up.

March 25, 1970

Since I last saw him, *A* has felt in top form, no troubles of any kind. With the ghost of a smile he says: "I have been thinking, you know, that perhaps from the start the whole thing was exaggerated. Maybe I pestered you without cause, if we're to be quite honest about it."

V: "Such pooh-poohing of bygone troubles is a commonplace with patients at the end of their treatment. In your case it is understandable in the setting of what, for the sake of brevity, we may call your problems of dominance and submission. That theme was present all the time, as you know, but its development was particularly noticeable in the final stage of your regular treatment. Keeping this in mind, we might rephrase your remark of a moment ago as follows: 'Now that I am well, I am naturally inclined to let you know that I doubt whether it was ever truly necessary for me to enter into a relationship of such dependent submissiveness as the one I established with you.' "

A (with a laugh): "OK, you hit the bull's-eye. I won't deny that to begin with I would have given anything just to be accepted for treatment."

We exchange these words at the end of the session. Before that he has spoken only of general subjects of interest to him.

April 6, 1970

A makes no mention of any symptoms; apparently he is free of them. He does, however, talk a good deal about feeling highly susceptible emotionally; in particular he is easily moved. He talks it over with me whether or not this is something new. He has always had a tendency in that direction, he says. A shift of emphasis, however, may have taken place, now that he no longer has any symptoms. He draws the conclusion himself that for the time being, instead of actual signs of illness, he experiences an accentuation of something normal: an excessive emotive propensity.

[103]

April 20, 1970

A arrives in a cheerful mood and in a state of well-being. He says that nowadays, truth to tell, he only sees me for the pleasure of it. Ever since last session he has felt fit as a fiddle. His annoying over-emotionalism waned too, after we had talked about it. He then tells me about his daughter being confirmed yesterday. After that he touches on the question of his professorship, of when the chair will be advertised. In this connection he mentions that it would not surprise him if N were to try to delay the establishment of the post—not out of any personal animosity; rather, N's policy is to hold onto qualified members of his staff, even to the detriment of their advancement. *A* also says in passing that after all there is no sure way of knowing that other qualified applicants, from Norway or Sweden for instance, won't turn up. Were it to come to that, he believes he would not feel all that disappointed having to stay at N's department, provided that he could have something along the lines of an associate professorship.

Having listened for some time to his qualms about this, I state as my considered opinion that his notions concerning the obstacles to his professorial appointment are not rational. It is not very likely that N should have the power to protract the creation of a chair, and his fear of competition from foreigners, whom he has no reason to believe are better qualified than he, makes just as little sense. Therefore I believe his meanderings reflect the remnants of his apprehension at the thought of sole leadership.

With seeming conviction he admits that I am probably right, and in that case the only sensible thing would be for him to confront N with what he regards as his just demands. The whole matter has been in N's hands; however, he has not done anything about it. Until now A has put up with that, but he acknowledges that his attitude is probably the wrong one.

I propose that we meet again four weeks from now, which he finds satisfactory. I add that if he runs into any problems of a factual kind—the sort we have just been discussing—which he finds difficulty in solving, he should just give me a ring; then we can meet and discuss them.

May 19, 1970

A arrives at the time we agreed upon. He remarks on the long lapse of time since we last saw each other. He has felt very well and has been free of his former symptoms. "Of course that doesn't mean that I haven't felt down a bit from time to time, but that had nothing to do with my symptoms." (He reverts to these fluctuations of mood towards the end of the session.)

He talks at some length about professional matters. Apparently nothing is happening in the case of his special department and professorship. He does not doubt that it would suit N fine if he were to stay in the department under N: It would accord well with his general policy of holding onto his people, even to the detriment their career. However he has now told N—and intends to go on doing so—that he must not count on his (A's) staying on in his present capacity in the future. If the professorship in question does not materialize, he will probably apply somewhere else. That would involve no difficulties worth mentioning and no financial loss at all.

Toward the end of the session A turns to discussing his domestic affairs. He says that at the time of our last talk he was convinced that his relationship with O had been the chief cause of the onset of his neurotic state. The reason for this conviction was in all probability that it was the last subject we dealt with, and that the elucidation of it brought about such a manifest amelioration of his condition. Shortly after his last session with me, however, he realized that, the importance of this notwithstanding, the prime factor was still to be found in his marital set-up, that is to say, in the discontent which springs from his and his wife's erotic life together. He acknowledged that this was a truth he had all along tried to deny, and that this denial in turn was a consequence of his former attitude toward marriage as such—that it should be a state of eternal bliss—an attitude very much due to his father's influence. The full realization he had now reached—that he could not honestly make that claim on behalf of his own marriage, however much he had tried to do so in the past—made him feel low for quite a while. In a general sense his marriage is, after all, mostly a success, and from a procreational point of view the sexual side of his life has been everything he could wish for—his problems are bound up with the purely erotic. When it comes to that, his wife has a whole set of firm, unshakeable convictions, and although he is willing to admit that it is his rightful duty to comply with her ideas to a large extent, he cannot help feeling that in return she ought to be amenable to some of his wishes: She too might change a little and yield a point or two. This, however, she seems unable to do. The more thought he gave to these matters, recognizing them as a vitally contributing cause of his anxiety states, the more his depression lifted, so that some two weeks ago he felt fully restored. He now consoles himself with the belief that a marriage serenely happy in all respects must be a rarity indeed.

(This realization of his I believe to be an important

one, since it seems to show that *A* is not prone to sec-
ondary repression of important conflict matter after the
termination of his treatment. That should to some degree guarantee the stability of the therapeutic result.)

In reply to my question of whether he wants to see me
again before the vacation or after, he says, judging from
how he feels, he sees no reason for coming until afterwards. Accordingly we decide that he can phone in the
middle of August. In this connection he expresses a certain joy at not having to sever his ties with me altogether.
He finds it is nice not to be left completely on his own.

June 9, 1970

A has taken advantage of my offer that, if necessary, he
might phone for an appointment anytime he liked before the start of the vacation.

Having turned up he immediately comes to the point:
He phoned because one night he experienced feelings of
anxiety, enough to remind him of old times. He did not
lose his head, however; nor did he let on to his wife. It
happened several days ago, and, properly speaking, his
need of seeing me has passed, since he himself discov-
ered what lay behind his anxiety and thus overcame it.

This is what happened: The day before they held a
birthday celebration in honor of N at the hospital, and *A*
was to give the speech. He decided to pepper it with a
few digs at N, humorous and acceptable in form, but in a
serious context. However, the whole thing misfired
completely, N cutting in then and there while *A* was
speaking and with quick repartees stultifying all his attacks. "And of course that was what troubled me, because while in relation to O I wear the pants, with N it is,
if anything, the other way around. What I did was an
attempt to change that, but he turned the tables on me."

He passes on to the prospects of getting his professorship. A delay seems inevitable, and he discerns unmistakable signs, he believes, that N would prefer someone from outside for the professorship in order to keep him (*A*) on as his chief medical assistant and lecturer. He speculates on whether he has really managed to convey to N that this is something he must not count on. If he does not get his chair, the inevitable result will be that he applies for a post elsewhere. I reinforce his belief in the importance of making it quite plain to N that he has nothing to gain by recruiting someone else as professor.

August 24, 1970

A arrives as we arranged now that the vacation is over. He starts by saying that he has been fine. He believes his neurotic condition to be a thing of the past. "Don't misconstrue that to mean I may never again feel anxiety. I do from time to time—actually always did, I think. But now it is under my firm control, I feel. I am nearly always able to pinpoint the incident that has triggered any such reaction on my part. In my daily life it troubles me not one whit. When I think of last summer, how truly grateful I am for the result!"

He tells me about a congress he attended in Japan and how he spent his holidays on Ceylon. It all came off very well. At her own request his wife accompanied him. Actually he would have preferred to go alone. He feels this need to be alone every now and then, but only seldom does he get the chance. His wife simply does not recognize this need for solitude and wants to be with him always. If he could have his way, he would like his own bedroom too; that, however, is out of the question, he says with a smile. Should he care to take a walk, his wife will usually accompany him, even if she is pressed for time. She is well-satisfied with the state he is in now—and says so. "It is like having received the gift of a new and better husband," is how she puts it. He did not question her as to what precisely she meant; but it is his guess it is probably that he is no longer finicky about such matters as dinner time.

This summer, between two of her periods, his wife bled a bit. It gave her a scare, and he too thought it might be cancer. "Now this is quite a confession to make," he says, "but I actually realized I was toying with the thought that this might mean my chance of getting rid of her. It was very salutary, I am sure, to be forced to face up to this alluring train of thought, because it also compelled me to weigh the good in our marriage against the bad. I came to the conclusion that without a doubt the good was very much preponderant."

He is calm and feels well; we agree that he should report to me in the beginning of November.

November 9, 1970

A phoned for an appointment as he wants to report according to our agreement. He is in good shape; he only feels a slight anxiety from time to time, especially upon waking up at night out of some frightening dream he cannot remember—"all this is scarcely worth mentioning, really." Towards the end of our talk, after discussing professional problems, of which more below, he returns to the anxious sensations. He feels that he owes me the admission, he says, that my original assertion was right about *coitus interruptus*—it is productive of anxiety. He became increasingly convinced to the truth of this and consequently began to use a sheath. Admittedly, this also involves a certain interference with the natural course of things; however, it certainly beats interrupted intercourse. He feels more satisfied afterwards and has noticed that such anxiety as may arise is now easier to control. In the course of our discussion he confirms that, because of his wife's loathing of being "sullied," he had to make the interruption a drastic one, in order to keep his emission from touching any part of her body, and that therefore she would not assist him in reaching actual ejaculation point. These are probably important factors in determining his preference for using a sheath. He adds that he takes pleasure in the thought that for all practical purposes he was able to master his anxiety while still living on the old system of *coitus interruptus*.

He also wants to discuss the following: His future professorship is on the priority list drawn up by the Ministry of Education, for which appropriation was expected. Now, however, he has learnt from N that possibly the Ministry of Finance will pass only a few of these applications and in consequence A just may not be included. N dropped his remark at lunchtime in the presence of others, without informing A in advance. A immediately replied that in that case he would have to look around for another job. In consequence the department staff overwhelmed him with earnest requests not to apply elsewhere.

Faced with the possibility of a deferment, he feels insecure about his future, among other things because it has become plainer and plainer to him that P definitely does not wish to see him made a professor. For one thing P fears that A may then dominate him; for another he is jealous of A's talents as a teacher and lecturer. His very real ability shows in the fact that at the students' request he had to move over to the large auditorium, where as many as 200 of them have gathered around him even so late into the term. In glaring contrast, P sits with a bare 25. *A* conveys his assertion about P's attitude in a very convincing manner. Now he realizes how stupidly he behaved when long ago he withdrew his application in favor of P. Earlier in our talk I had suggested the possibility of changing the order on the list of priorities. He replied that such a maneuver would imply improving his own status at the expense of another man. I recall this remark, interpreting it as yet another expression of his anti-aggressive proclivities. Although at first noncommittal, he seems struck by what I say.

I ask *A* to give me a ring as soon as he has any news of his professorship.

November 10, 1970

A phones me today to tell me that he has talked to both N and P, that they are both very sympathetically inclined towards his appointment as professor, and that he seems to have misjudged P's attitude. Moreover the entire scientific staff of the department has made a joint move in his support, petitioning the ministry for the establishment of a new department and a professorship for him. He feels great satisfaction at the reactions he has met on all sides.

CODA

Until recently, my contacts with *A*, who became a professor, have been few and far between during the many years that have gone by since I completed the last entry. We have talked together on the phone thrice in contexts not connected with his illness, and once, a good many years ago, I ran into him abroad by pure luck. Each time, not unnaturally, I asked him how he was doing, and he invariably answered that he was well and had been so ever since we parted.

A'S COMMENTARY,
SEVENTEEN YEARS AFTER

I have been completely well all these years since the end
of my treatment.

Vanggaard turned out to be a little older than I, a man
with a friendly, somewhat distant smile, quiet hands,
courteous and correct. He came to the point at once, in
a way inspiring confidence, restrained, professional, but
also revealing personal warmth. Already after a few minutes of talking it was clear to me that this was a man by
whom I would like to be treated. I noted two things in
particular. Vanggaard let fall a casual remark to the effect
that you don't die from your attacks of panic. That was
precisely the danger I believed to be imminent. Small
wonder I felt moved; it was only with difficulty that I
was able to stammer out my thanks for his readiness to
take me into treatment. On the other hand, the condition set by Vanggaard—for my own sake, as he said—

scared me. I was not to take any kind of psychopharma-cological drugs at all, but meprobamate to go to sleep. For a second I did not trust my own ears, but he said it as though it were a matter of course and plainly counted on my ability to go through with it. Consequently I at once made up my mind to obey.

Up till then I had, for quite a long time, been consuming large quantities of chlorpromazine (a neuroleptic drug), prescribed by my general practitioner. Incidentally, laying off this drug proved quite easy; it felt rather like liberation, a return to life. The only effect the drug had had was that some of my colleagues found me somehow changed. It did not quell my panic. I should also add that my neurosis did not otherwise impinge upon those around me, except of course during the times I was in the hospital and the lengthy holidays I took on the advice of my physician. My excuse was overwork.

During the days before I went into analysis I was nagged by two fears: One was that a person who obviously did not share my lifelong religious convictions should by his influence lead me to betray those convictions. The other was a totally irrational fear of being forced to do something sexually perverted. Try as I might to persuade myself that this fear was utterly groundless, it never left me until the treatment was well under way.

Finally I blamed myself for not having given Vang-gaard a true picture of my feelings of being in hell. I only mentioned my fear of dying. There *is* such a thing as an abysmal terror which is incapable of verbal expression. I do not think that I ever, at any point in my analysis, succeeded in putting it into words. The doctor's notes convey but a pale reflection of the nameless dread I had to live through during the months before my illness was correctly diagnosed and treatment begun.

[114]

My treatment was a positive experience through and through. At first that came simply from the reassurance that my death was not imminent. But also, more important still, what made it so was the sense of being in good hands, with a person who had my well-being at heart and who was a competent professional. Here and there Vanggaard talks of the attacks of panic, massive and concrete, which I sustained, as *reactions to the treatment*. I saw them as a continuation of my illness, although decreasing in its intensity. Vanggaard's urgent admonitions to go on with the treatment were superfluous, really. For a long time I had too many attacks of panic, albeit somewhat attenuated, to contemplate a return to the horrors of my neurosis by giving up treatment.

Never believe that psychotherapy turns life into a fool's paradise. If you are just seeking comfort and a relaxed mind, you had better, I think, choose another way. My life continues sufficiently tempestuous, but I have learned to steer so that I am capable of wrestling with the things I come up against without stifling with fear.

Immediately upon finishing analysis I felt full of energy and threw myself into political activity. My talent for speedily writing letters, speeches, and reports led me to a position of trust within the party. On several occasions I achieved personal triumphs by wielding my talent for stripping an adversary or a rival bare and making him look ridiculous. However, I also found that the joy won through victories of that sort is but fleeting. In the long run you sow hatred and reap opposition, especially among people who do not have the knack of hitting back with the same hearty brutality. Furthermore, I became progressively conscious that the ideology of the party really was not my cup of tea. It had to come to a parting. And I regret some of the things I did during that

[115]

period, in an excess of activity that was the result, or so I think, of my reprieve from the paralysis caused by my anxiety.

Looking back now after 17 years, after due consideration I believe that my neurosis sprang from two sources: one a religious crisis, the other conflicts in connection with aggression—of anger and the wielding of power—which Vanggaard uncovered in my relationships with my wife and with other men. (Perhaps, after all, the religious part is not all that easily distinguished from my other conflicts, especially when you consider my relationship with my father.) But I want to address the religious concern. Any way you look at it, my religious outlook was of prime importance to me. Even two or three years after I was cured, I was haunted by troublesome religious scruples. I might be folding my hands to pray; then it would come as a lightning revelation: No, God is angry with you, and you are heading for hell. My fear was thus explicitly cast in a religious mold: I had to grapple with this fear, rephrasing that horrible sentence over and over. Only thus could I take it out of its context, analyze its origin and content, assess the truth of it—finally to discard it with a triumphant smile. So the story ends. But not in bliss: Many unsolved problems remain.

As regards my religious crisis, the first point I would make is that the Mission is a firm anchorage for a good many people, especially those who have the flexibility to hold onto individual, nonconformist views while yet retaining the common bond. This was beyond my abilities. Thanks to my father I grew up with the Gospel, but also with the belief that the unconverted were the damned. This belief I have had to pull myself loose from. I no longer believe in the existence of two classes of humans. That means that we all carry responsibility for one another and hold power over one another for good or evil. Among missionaries of my father's stripe you are not responsible, at most you are instrumental. And when you harbor thoughts and emotions and have done deeds for which you cannot take full responsibility, the result is fear, because there is nowhere to turn to for forgiveness.

Through my treatment I learned that responsibility is personal, most of the time at any rate, and that this means that you can shoulder your responsibility. Thus you are not powerless against your fear or other emotions: Your thoughts, emotions, and deeds are a burden you must carry yourself. But forgiveness is possible. This worked a change in my religious outlook, and thus I was finally set free from my anxiety.

It is six o'clock in the morning, and it is dark outside my windows. Soon it will be Christmas. The boy who brings my morning paper is at the garden gate. He drives a Suzuki 700, which he has left with the motor running at the curb in an attempt to wake up the whole neighborhood. He even has a stereo radio mounted on the steering wheel. It plays at full blast pop or rock music as a rule, but today a school choir is singing: "Infant Jesus in a manger lay/ though his heritage was Heaven." The young fellow walks down my garden row, and they reach the lines: "We shall enter this child's presence/ and become in soul and mind as children too."

This is really too much, so he changes to another and more up-to-date program. I do understand him. It is all nonsense. Hans Christian Andersen was balmy, you cannot believe in that sort of thing. Senseless. But delightful too. Maybe I cannot live without it—and maybe I do not have to either.

Annotations

INTRODUCTORY NOTE

It is widely held that psychoanalysis is a process spanning two to four years, or longer, involving three to four sessions a week. And that is frequently the case. But analyses of shorter duration with good results do exist. The treatment of *A*, consisting as it did of three weekly sessions regularly for just over five and a half months and sporadic sessions spread out over the following six months, was thus shorter than most successful analyses, but it was an analysis nonetheless. There was no way of knowing from the start that so comparatively short a time would prove sufficient. The specific mark of a psychoanalysis, as opposed to other kinds of treatment, is that *it aims at uncovering unconscious intrapsychic conflict*. The implications of that fundamental function and the means used to achieve the goal are briefly expounded in the following on the basis of *A*'s treatment,

[121]

which was planned and conducted on the lines of a classical psychoanalysis.

First I shall deal with the diagnosis and the psychodynamic understanding of such a condition as *A*'s.

Diagnosis

When *A* first came to see me, his condition for the last two to three months had been one of severe suffering. One can experience few things more painful than such attacks of panic. The panic, with the concomitant heart symptoms, seemed so frightening that even a man as knowledgeable and otherwise self-controlled as *A* was unable to keep his head. He called for a doctor or an ambulance. In his commentary above *A* himself described the horror of his panic together with the sense of sin and guilt which in his mortal terror weighed him down.

When I began this case record, I classified *A*'s sufferings as manifestations of an anxiety neurosis of the type now called *panic disorder*. His condition was thus a *neurotic* one. And the precise content of the word *neurosis* calls for clarification, since this word is used in a loose and fuzzy sense by nonprofessionals and often, alas, by medical men too. It is wrong to do so. The term neurosis may, nay *must*, be given a reasonably clear, sharp characterization.* *A*'s condition may be used to

---

*The word "reasonably" is not used in order to weaken the statement in any way. It simply means that clarity and sharpness can be maintained only to the limit set of a necessity by the fact that the beings dealt with are living, individual humans. Their characteristics are not definable in the true Aristotelian sense of the term. They may be classified, through description, according to their discernible properties and thus delimited from others on grounds of differences.

demonstrate what is characteristic of any such neurotic condition.

What naturally follows is to delimit the category in question from two others: physical and mental illness. Despite his alarming heart symptoms *A* suffered from no *physical* illness, as was proved by the repeated and thorough medical examinations he went through during the first months of his ailment. Nor was it a case of mental illness in the sense of *madness*: Those about him took him, as a matter of course, to be normal in his general judgment, behavior, emotions, and matter of thought.

However, his dramatic main symptom—panic—is not specific to neurotic conditions. It may be found in identical form with depressive states as the phenomenon overshadowing all others. At the onset of schizophrenia and in the case of so-called schizophrenic borderline states one may meet with a display of panic which is easily mistaken for its neurotic counterpart. Discrimination is only possible by taking into consideration other aspects of the patient's condition and his general personality.

Anxiety neurotics invariably show striking common traits: Among these a dominant one is anti-aggressiveness. *A* felt a dislike for any show of antagonism in his immediate surroundings—this would actually disturb his peace of mind—and he found it difficult to put his foot down in any direct personal confrontation, even when it was a case of legitimate self-assertion or of the necessary reprimand of a subordinate. Nor could he stand hearing or reading about violence, cruelty, or bloody events; it even rubbed him the wrong way to watch his children playing cops and robbers.

All in all he impressed one as a person with whom it was easy to establish an emotional relationship, although his emotional appeal was tactful and unobtrusive. In this he differed from most anxiety neurotics, who will foist their agony on you with dramatic, emotionally demanding intensity. A was not like that; he was among those who are capable of handling an anxiety neurotic temperament with discretion.

Finally, like any neurotic personality, A had no knowledge at all of what it was in his mind that caused his anxiety. With typically neurotic rationalization he regarded the somatic symptoms which went with his anxiety—palpitations and other sensations of the heart—as its basic cause. He knew nothing about the violent emotional forces which brought on his attacks of panic. They were safeguarded in the unconscious part of his mind and only saw the light of day as a result of treatment. His effective repressive ability is a fundamental characteristic of neurotic states. This is a specific difference from schizophrenic borderline states and certain forms of perversion, where repression is defective.

Psychodynamics

By dynamics is meant the interplay of forces, together and against one another. The dynamics in A's mind, which resulted in his attacks of panic, emerged clearly in the course of his analysis. Basically they belonged to two spheres: his relationship with his wife, and his relationship with his father and other men. In the final analysis *aggression* proved to be the dynamic factor which interfered with these relationships and which was responsible for his symptoms of panic as well as for his habitually anti-aggressive character.

The frustration to which he was subject every month during his wife's premenstrual period increasingly became a strain on him. They had both come to realize that a connection might exist between this and his attacks of panic so that they might be expected to occur during this period. According to Freud's original theory, this panic was triggered by "products of the sexual metabolism," which were accumulated in the body, he thought, when full orgastic satisfaction was not achieved. Freud abandoned this theory in favor of another, which he proposed in 1920. To put it briefly, he saw panic as a reaction upon strong tension due to dammed-up sexual drive. The theory about accumulated sexual body substances was thus replaced by the idea of dammed-up psychic sexual energy as the factor triggering panic. But still, frustrated sexual satisfaction was seen as directly productive of panic. This point of view would still seem to prevail.

Observations made in cases like A's—in my experience his case is by no means singular—seem to indicate the need for a modification of the theory. *It is proved that A rid himself of his panic without any changes in his marital relations*. This alone is fatal to the theory of sexual frustration—in his case, at any rate. I do not think it is tenable in general, either.

The explanation of his panic is a different one. If one follows the chain of events from beginning to end, it becomes apparent that what was so abhorrent to A was the *anger* he felt at the measure of sexual frustration he had to live with. That was what called forth his panic. This anger was unacceptable to him both because of his general anti-aggressive character and temperament and because it was at loggerheads with his love for his wife and his wish to be considerate to her. Thus, what was *directly* responsible for his attacks of panic was not frustrated libido, it was his aggressive reactions to libidinous frustration. Panic was his reaction to his own aggression.

[125]

Throughout the account it is possible to follow, in many-sided detail, the workings of his relationship with his father and other men, among them me. It is plain how full of conflict these relationships were. And here again, aggression is the main source of conflict.

His father he loved and admired—with good reason. All the same he reacted against him with protest—with good reason too. And he feared him. As is plainly clear, he saw his father as both God and the Devil. Naturally this made for conflicts in his relationship with both his father and his God.

This made itself directly felt in his relations with those who were then his superiors. Conversely, it set its mark on his emotional response to younger colleagues and to his son. This showed not least in his dreams. He harbored a wish to wield power over these people, even to make them the target of unbridled violence and destruction. As with all men the antiphonal nature of male dominance and submission found its expression in sexual symbols which are—in our civilization at any rate—in themselves controversial, particularly because such symbolism is always to some extent coupled with emotion.

In his relation to me his conflicts in this field mostly expressed themselves as a fear lest I should exploit my position by influencing him in ways he did not wish. This fear he voiced in a most pointed manner in the dream he had towards the end of the analysis: He did not want to emerge from the process as some mass-produced result along Freudian lines.

He had buried his aggressive feelings towards his wife, his father, and other men so effectively in the depths of his unconscious that they did not disturb his view of life as he wished it to be. He paid for this gain with symptoms of panic and the inhibitions imposed by his anti-aggressive character.

The three main psychic means he used to rid his mind of disturbing thoughts and emotions were: repression, denial, and reaction formation.

Repression is a psychic measure, unknown in nature, but well-known in its effects, by which thoughts and emotions are banished from the conscious mind and kept out. *A* had a vast capacity for repression. He showed this not least in the phenomenon, most unusual with a normal male, that clear until the end of his twenties he was conscious of no sexual desire. Otherwise this is only seen with men of weak drives, and *A* was, as it later proved, certainly not weak of drive.

But then, his general capacity for repression was enormous.

Denial means that you actually know that you think or feel in such and such a way, but that you deny its importance. At the beginning of the treatment, when we discussed the importance of being satisfied sexually, *A* plainly demonstrated his proclivity for denial.

Reaction formation means that, in order to keep an emotion repressed, you overstress its counterpart. Thus, if you want to repress lust for power, anger, inclinations to violence, or other aggressive propensities, you over-accentuate the opposite qualities: You fan your tender feelings, your care, and your consideration—as *A* did so palpably in many of his relationships.

The psychodynamics in the case of *A*'s anxiety neurotic state were a tug-of-war between aggression on the one hand and the so-called defenses on the other. Just as for many preceding years he had demonstrated his capacity for repressing his libido without suffering any consequences, so it played no leading part, dynamically,

[127]

in his neurosis. Only in its frustration did it trigger his panic-provoking aggression.

As progressively he acknowledged the existence of these conflicts and in the course of the analysis relived them, he was able to come to grips with them by means of his own psyche, thus controlling and changing them so that at first they decreased in intensity and in the end they disappeared. Thereby the forces previously tied up in conflict and anxiety were let loose—as *A* himself notes in his commentary. And thus he had to go through a period of trial and error.

Let it be noted that, judging from the course and content of the analysis, *A*'s mother played no part worth mentioning in the origin and maintenance of his neurosis, nor was she responsible for the development of the kind of character which was, so to speak, the soil from which his neurosis grew. It would be incorrect to draw the inference from this that she was of no importance in his life. But she did not give him cause for internal psychic conflict. That role his father preempted.

THE ANALYTICAL MEANS

The account of *A*'s analysis, as well as his comments on it, clearly demonstrate the fundamental character of any psychoanalysis: It is an emotional process. It is carried onward by the emotions of the patient in all their nuances and degrees of force, at times very strong ones. These emotions keep the process going; without them no analysis would be possible.

Correspondingly, a certain empathy is required on the part of the analyst. He must be able, intuitively and with sympathetic understanding, to sense within himself an echo of the emotions voiced by the patient. On the other hand, this emotional echo must be kept in a low key. The analyst must not let himself be carried away by any strong emotional response to his patient, be it positive or negative. That would slant his view and upset the balance of his judgment.

All this implies that neither analyst nor analysand works by the use of subtle intellectual powers. The necessary reasoning and the conclusions drawn are intellectually simple and fall within the province of common sense. This is borne out by my report on *A*'s case. Speculation, intellectualizing, is ruinous to an analysis while it is going on, and this goes for both parties involved. Theorizing is out of place during analysis. Analysts have evolved quite elaborate, subtle theories about the workings of the mind under normal and pathological conditions. But both parties to the analysis would do better to forget all about them during the sessions. As the reader may see for himself, I did not at any time theorize in my comments to *A*. Emotion and discursive reason are *complementary* functions in Niels Bohr's sense of the term. The moment you begin to speculate about your emotions intellectually they lose in intensity; they may even disappear, thus making analytical work impossible.

As with any successful analysis it was possible in *A*'s case to discern two distinct aspects of his emotional relationship with me: a *trust*, which was fundamental to our mutual therapeutic alliance, and *transference*.

The basic *trust* established itself already from our first encounter. This is apparent in *A*'s comments too, and it remained unaltered throughout the duration of the treatment, despite the doubts and misgivings he had to come to terms with again and again.

I on my part had a corresponding, unshakable feeling that *A* was a person I liked and with whom I felt able to cooperate. Without such a feeling it is unwise to attempt to carry out a psychoanalysis. After all, the analyst's situation is not at all the same as the surgeon's. While performing *his* main therapeutic work the surgeon deals with an unconscious person whose personality in waking life does not concern him.

Transference

By this is understood the circumstance that in his reactions to his analyst, the patient repeats feelings, ideas, and attitudes deriving from his life with others, mainly those holding a key position in his personal past.

In A's case transference was manifest from the very beginning. As he himself states, his spontaneous confidence in me immediately became mixed up with an anxious feeling that I might take advantage of my position by meddling with his religion and with his relationship with his wife. In any event both emerged as pivotal problems in his analysis, and in both cases aspects of his relationship with his forceful father were reenacted. These manifestations of transference might be followed through the analytical process ad nauseam; they are obvious, once one becomes aware of the phenomenon. Transference shows not least in connection with situations involving dominance and submision. These problems are always found where relations between men are hierarchic—and a therapeutic relationship is invariably felt as such by the patient. As demonstrated earlier, A's father transference showed directly in relation to his hierarchic superiors, and also, in inverted fashion, to his underlings.

Transference in its strictest and truest sense is limited to the relationship of the patient with his analyst. It is, however, only a special case of a basic property of all neurotics: *They are frozen in repetitive stereotypes.* The result of this is that relationships and circumstances are not dealt with as they would be seen by an unbiased mind, but rather as if they were shaped by the person's neurotic mode of experience. That is to say, they are determined by those rigid patterns of emotion and thought which form the distinct character and tempera-

[131]

ment of the person, inculcated through his development. However, with neurotics the stereotypes never cross the border into madness.

A's repetitive tendencies, as well in his bent for establishing overemotional relations with other people, were obvious.

Resistance

This is the phenomenon which occurs when a patient interrupts his free, uncensured communication of thoughts and feelings to the analyst. It may take the form of his stopping short as he is speaking, or he may begin to talk about neutral subjects as a cover-up for something else. A showed both forms of resistance. He stopped short and felt anxiety before he could pick up the courage to speak to me about his religion, and time and again he would resort to "filling in pauses," as he himself called it, when he wanted to avoid broaching some subject.

Resistance is healthy in itself and is only to be deplored in the sad cases when a patient clams up completely. But when the patient is capable of overcoming his resistance, as A was, the surmounting of obstacles always means a forward step therapeutically.

Dreams

A great deal of our mental life is dream life. Every normal person experiences four or five dream periods each night. Taken together they occupy about an hour and a half of the total time he sleeps, that is to say, on the average a little more than a fifth of it. During these periods the electric activity in the brain, as recorded in an electroencephalogram, differs decisively from that recorded during dreamless sleep and in the waking state.

The three conditions—dream sleep (D-sleep), dreamless sleep (S-sleep), and waking life—are so different that many authorities would regard them as three quite different forms of human existence.

During the periods of dream sleep a person's general state differs from that of his dreamless sleep. Quick movements of the eyes occur: great variations in pulse, blood pressure, and breathing; with men partial or full erections; and general muscular relaxation, interrupted by sudden, brief contractions of isolated groups of muscles. Contrary to what one would expect, sleep is deepest during the dream periods, at least if depth of sleep is measured by how hard it is to awake the sleeper.

People dream whether they remember their dreams or not. In this respect variations are wide. But even those who habitually do not remember their dreams may accustom themselves to doing so, if they turn their attention to it immediately upon waking.

In the daily life of our civilization dreams have lost status. Lost is the right word here, for in other times and other cultures dreams have been taken very seriously. With good reason: In dream life aspects of a person's mental life emerge which are totally or partially unknown to himself. Dreams may also admonish, warn, or—as Heraclitus said of the Delphic oracle—give a sign, point out a direction.

In dreams you hallucinate. Vision and sensation predominate, hearing somewhat less so. However, a sound in a dream may be so loud as to actually wake up the dreamer. But, by and large, the performance on our inner stage is one of visions and feelings, impressions as strong as any we ever know, some people even claim that the panic or orgastic gratification—to mention two sensations poles asunder—which they experience while dreaming surpass anything they know from their waking life.

[133]

Although our dreams impress us so vividly as *real*, they have at the same time the additional quality that the dependence on empirical and logical laws known to us from our waking life is here utterly suspended. Time— before and after, simultaneousness and sequence— place, size, weight, space, gravity, the correlation of parts, the relation of the part to the whole, all such matters are no longer valid. Emotion is the sole supreme arbiter of everything. The freedom thus reigning in the world of dreams is precisely what makes for its wide range of expressive possibility.

It was Freud who was to elucidate the nature and function of dreams in 1900, in his great work *The Interpretation of Dreams*, epoch-making and exhaustive as it was.

Whatever is peculiar and proper to dream life was succinctly described in a sonnet by the brilliant Confederate gentleman and poet Sidney Lanier, who died 19 years before the publication of *The Interpretation of Dreams*:

Swift, through some trap mine eyes have never found
Dim-paneled in the painted scene of Sleep,
Thou, giant Harlequin of Dreams, does leap
Upon my spirit's stage. Then Sight and Sound,
Then Space and Time, then Language, Mete and Bound,
And all familiar Forms that firmly keep
Man's reason in the road, change faces, peep
betwixt the legs, and mock the daily round.
Yet thou canst more than mock: sometimes my tears
At midnight break through bounden lids—a sign
Thou hast a heart; and oft thy little leaven
Of dream-taught wisdom works me bettered years;
In one night witch, saint, trickster, fool divine,
I think thou'rt Jester at the Court of Heaven.

[134]

In another poem, entitled "The Marshes of Glynn,"
Lanier's final stanza runs:

And now from the Vast of the Lord will the waters of sleep
Roll in on the souls of men,
But who will reveal to our waking ken
The forms that swim and the shapes that creep
Under the waters of sleep?
And I would I could know what swimmeth below when
    the tide comes in
On the length and the breadth of the marvellous marshes
    of Glynn.

Two decades were to pass before the man came who
took it upon himself to reveal what swims and creeps
under the waters of sleep.

The case report is in itself witness to the important
part *A*'s dreams played in his analysis. *A* was a good
dreamer. That is to say, his dreams were concise and they
fitted well into the inner and outer pattern of his life
during the period when we saw each other regularly.

My case report shows that I never interpret a dream in
isolation. No gauge exists for the correct interpretation
of dreams, nor have we any lexicon where, by simple
reference, we may find the key to the means of expression utilized in dreams. To me dreams are always part of
a whole, and that is how I use them analytically. The
components of this whole are partly what other events
may occur in the life of the patient, partly what takes
place during the actual analytical sessions, in particular
the one in which the dream is recounted; in addition,
the analysand's relationship with me—his transference,
that is—and finally, his emotions, thoughts, and recollections in general must be taken into consideration. The
ideas and feelings called up in me enter into it too. Thus

[135]

in the end the dream forms part of a larger entity, whose other components contribute to an understanding of the entire situation. I never endeavor to interpret a dream out of context. This case report contains instances of dreams which I found intelligible even though I did not offer any interpretation because I could not find an ideational whole into which it fit.

Any dream of *A*'s would serve as demonstration of how I work with dreams. Take the dream he recounted the 23rd of February: He was in bed with his wife, had an erect penis of inordinate size and was about to demonstrate what wonders he could work with it. But then four orderlies took his bed and, despite his furious protests, carried him away in it. One of them he could not see, because he was behind the head of the bed; that was me, he believed. His wife suddenly was not there anymore. Now he saw the bed, with himself in it, being carried down a corridor; but he was transformed into an impersonal, oblong object, regularly, neatly, and precisely cut into eight parts, crosswise and lengthwise.

A's spontaneous reaction to his dream was that it expressed his fear of losing his personal identity and turning into what I felt a human being should be like. This accords with his comment that in the days between our preliminary discussion and the start of the treatment he was haunted by a fear that I should try to make him change against his own convictions. This fear of his came out in the open when, five weeks later, on October 24th, he stopped short during a session, had an attack of panic with palpitations of the heart, and in the following discussion admitted that he had been afraid of talking to me about his religious life, afraid that I should interfere with it. This revelation and demonstration against having to submit to me and my demand for complete frankness resulted immediately afterwards in a violent attack of panic, which occurred at a meeting with the two professors who were his superiors, and the accompanying heart symptoms were so severe that the instruments in his breast pocket rattled.

Thus A took his dream to be a manifestation of his fear of having to give up his masculinity and independence and of being cast in the mold of what he thought were my Freudian preconceptions. Moreover, he immediately went on to speak about a book I had lent him, claiming that never earlier in his life would he have ventured to read a book expressing such a philosophy of life, for fear that it might disturb the kind of religious outlook with which he was raised. Thus, in connection with his account of his dream, he immediately once again referred to his misgivings about my influence and, intertwined with this, alluded to the way he had let his personality be shaped by his father's overbearing piety. It was an obvious manifestation of transference, a mix-up of his father and me. Thereby his conflicts of submission were alerted to such a degree that they made themselves felt forcibly in an encounter with his two superiors. It was apparent that he was working over his problems of dominance and submission and, as it proved, clarifying them. In this process his dream and situations within and outside of the analytic sessions supplemented one another.

His relationship with his assistant O—who, for quite a long time and notably during the past week, had figured in his accounts and dreams—was part of the same pattern. As a corollary to mentioning the problems he was having with O, he for instance had the dramatic and illuminating dream, related on February 16th, in which he ran O down with a bus, mauling him badly. This entire material could now be utilized for a thorough discussion of his relationships with other men, subordinates and superiors, in which dreams joined with the other elements to create a comprehensible pattern.

Continuity

No therapeutic process can claim to be a psychoanalysis unless the sessions are so connected that material dealt with demonstrably produces an effect in the intervals between them; this also means that subject matter from one session should reappear in the next. That is apparent throughout this account. Continuity is the reason for the necessity of seeing the patient regularly several times a week. For analysis proper three times a week with one day's interval—as in *A*'s case—is the minimum. Starting tentatively with three weekly sessions, I was prepared to raise the number to four, if necessary. It proved not to be. On the contrary, I believe that in *A*'s case three was the optimum number, seeing that he cooperated as fruitfully as he did.

Interpretation

It should be apparent how I used interpretation. I would only call attention to the fact that no interpretation was ever offered before some manifestation of the subject in question had showed up in relation to me, in the transference that is.

Childhood

Every human being carries his personal history with him at all times. Past and present form a synthesis in our every thought, emotion, action, and dream. Every part of *A*'s story, as we have come to know it, bears witness to this. The account is full of examples; not only his immediate surroundings and their influence on him, but even dreams and fantasies all the way back to his childhood years set their stamp on him as a mature adult.

To no small extent man's destiny is under his own control. This was an insight *A* won. And that this is so is precisely what offered him the possiblility of working his way out of his neurotic condition. Forces within himself established his neurotic state in an attempt to resolve conflict, but just as truly his own inner dynamic reserves enabled him to break out of the neurosis again. For, in the last resort, he was his own healer. The analyst's rightful claim is only to the roles of companion, helper—catalyst. Here again one sees the immense difference between somatic treatment and treatment of the psyche such as this.

As human beings we are thus a synthesis of our own potential on the one hand and the influence of our surroundings on the other. Already in the fetal state plural forces are probably at work: genes and all else that govern the growth and development of the fetus, but also influences from the mother about which we know little. After birth the child's congenital equipment and its own spontaneous physical and psychic development interact constantly with its surroundings, and foremost with its parents.

However much one may disagree with the outlook on life which prevailed in the home of *A*'s parents and with which he grew up, one should not overlook that, despite his critical attitude, *A* looked back on his childhood home with gratitude and was happy about the relaxed relationship he, with the help of analysis, could establish with his father. Moreover, he did very well indeed

[139]

in life in general and experienced nothing disturbing enough to make him seek medical aid before he was approaching his middle forties. Add to this that he was able to work his way out of his neurosis with the aid of an analysis which was certainly not lengthy measured by common standards. The late appearance of his symptoms, coupled with the successful and durable result of his analysis, shows that his personality was well-functioning and well-knit. It is worthy of note that while an upbringing such as his may produce inhibitions and restrictions, the stability of its values also contributes to the building up of a correspondingly stable personality.

A background of stable values is probably a prerequisite for ordering unsolved conflicts through the development of a neurosis. And, when desperate means are to be resorted to, such a development is preferable by far, for both the person himself and his surroundings, to the discharge of conflict through psychopathy or drug addiction. The latter two are seen more commonly where the childhood home was marked by excessive tolerance, loose or conflicting values—or none at all.

Thus, *A*'s ability to rid himself of his neurosis was rooted not merely in inherent individual strength; discipline had done its work as well.

Finally, one should always keep in mind that what emerges in analysis about parents is only the conflicts and disturbances they engendered, not the benefits they bestowed.

Steering the Analytical Process

As already noted, the analysand himself does the better part of the therapeutic work. The role of the analyst is at best like that of a midwife. Take a look at the respective roles of the patient and the analyst.

The patient has the leading part. It is he who decides the subjects to be taken up. In a successful treatment the patient will touch on his main conflicts in one form or another from the very start, as *A* did.

During his first session he mentioned his relationships with his wife and, indirectly, his father.

You may look at the second and third sessions in two ways. They contain an interesting recital of conditions in a developing country and of the interference of white men with foreign cultures. They are also steeped in information about how much his father influenced his attitude toward life and guided his actions, but about his counter-reactions too, for instance about how he wriggled out of the whole missionary business. In the end, of course, this led to his important working out of his relationships with his father and other men.

During the fourth session he spoke out about the specific element of frustration in his relations with his wife.

Within both main spheres covered by these initial four sessions one senses the outlines of aggressive tensions which later, in their ramifications, were to become the main theme of the analysis. But it is *A* who brings up these matters, and continuously in every session he decides to what subjects he will devote his—and my—time. And *he* starts off the sessions—always.

The analyst's part is to listen, be attentive, and react when he feels it to be appropriate. Reactions on his part may be, for instance, indications of self-contradictions and inconsistencies, as exemplified by my provocative remarks about the method of birth control. The analysand may then react immediately; he may also begin the next session by saying that my remarks last time "caused him turmoil" or made him "grumpy." This obviously influenced the course of things, but what is influenced is always something the patient has started himself. The same goes for interpretation and explanatory summing up. The analyst's reactions may annoy and provoke, and thus stimulate the analytical process. In this the analyst resembles Socrates when he called himself a gadfly sent to keep the Athenian people from dozing off. Instances of this abound in the analysis of *A*. At other times the effect of interpretations and explanations is clarifying and soothing.

The analyst may regard his efforts with the analysand as successful if he can say with Kierkegaard's Justice Vilhelm at the end of his second letter to Johannes: "While you labor on yourself within the closed machinery of your individuality I stick in my contributions and make sure they are taken up in the motion of the process."

PSYCHIATRIC EPILOGUE

In the introductory part of this book I mentioned that panic states may, symptomatically, appear to be identical whether they rise from a *neurotic* condition or from a *manic-depressive* one. However, the first type of panic should be treated with psychotherapy without the use of drugs, as in *A*'s case, while manic-depressive states are to be treated with one of our effective antidepressive drugs. The two groups are differentiated by considering the general personalities and case histories of the patients.

However, lately influential circles in the United States have fostered the preposterous idea of abolishing the category of neurosis. States resembling *A*'s, all and sundry, are huddled together in one heap called "Panic Disorder." Allegedly they are all to be treated with antidepressive drugs. This provoked strong counter-reactions in the USA—which again resulted in a miserable compromise. But in many quarters, and also in Europe, the efforts to do away with the diagnosis of neurosis left an impression on many psychiatrists.

From *A*'s story, including our knowledge of its outcome, it may safely be deduced that his condition was determined by his psyche and that it could, and should, have been treated by purely psychic means. It was what, since Freud, we have always called a neurosis. Conceptually it would have been senseless and the consequences would have been detrimental had he been wrongly diagnosed and given antidepressive treatment. Such treatment would certainly not have freed him of his panic—and with equal certainty would have afflicted him with the violent and most unpleasant side-effects antidepressive drugs have on everyone who does not have the disposition of the manic-depressive.

The explanation of the conceptually misleading American attack on the diagnosis of neurosis is a simple one. The fact is that the psychiatrists who worked for the introduction of a diagnostic system free of neuroses—called *DSM-III, DSM-III-R*—are hospital psychiatrists. *And hospital psychiatrists never see any neurotics.* In private practice I myself, for some years in New York and for many in Copenhagen, encountered many patients with panic, neurotics as well as manic-depressives. But during my nearly 20 years at the psychiatric department of the University Hospital of Copenhagen I recall the admission of only one anxiety neurotic. She was a young woman, who had been brought by an ambulance to the emergency ward with heart symptoms and fear of dying; the sum of symptoms she displayed was quite similar to *A*'s. She was sent on to the psychiatric department, and then immediately released for ambulatory treatment with me. She was treated with psychotherapy without the use of drugs. Her treatment was less thorough than *A*'s, although it lasted longer. She has done well and after 25 years still holds a responsible post; her children developed excellently too.

The intensive study of single cases is not prominent in psychiatric literature nowadays. It is a pity, because from studies of single patients we have always drawn our most valuable knowledge.